From Access to Power

FROM ACCESS TO POWER
Black Politics in Boston

Edited by
James Jennings
and
Mel King

Introduction by
Hubert E. Jones

Schenkman Books, Inc.
Cambridge, Massachusetts

Copyright © 1986

Schenkman Books, Inc.
190 Concord Avenue
P.O. Box 1570
Cambridge, Massachusetts 02138

Library of Congress Cataloging-in-Process Data

Jennings, James and King, Mel
    From Access to Power

  Includes index.
  1. Afro-Americans—Boston (Mass.)—Politics and suffrage—Addresses, essays, lectures. 2. Boston (Mass.)—Race relations—Addresses, essays, lectures. 3. Boston (Mass.)—Politics and government—Addresses, essays, lectures. I. Jennings, James, 1949-
II. King, Mel.
F73.9.N4F76   1986   323.1′196073′074461   85-30291
ISBN 0-87047-021-3
ISBN 0-87047-020-5 (pbk.)

Printed in the United States of America

All rights reserved. This book, or parts thereof, may not be reproduced in any form without written permission from publisher.

Table of Contents

Preface 1

Introduction by Hubert E. Jones 3

PART ONE: *Race and Politics in Boston, 1900-1983* 9

I   Black Politics in Boston, 1900-1950
           James Jennings 11

II   Three Stages of Black Politics in
           Boston, 1950-1980
           Melvin I. King 23

III   Race, Class and Politics in the
           Black Community of Boston
           James Jennings 39

IV   Urban Machinism and the Black Voter:
           The Kevin White Years
           James Jennings 57

PART TWO: *The Mel King for Mayor Campaigns, 1979 and 1983*

V   Boston: Chaos or Community?
           Mel King and James Jennings 89

VI   The Making of Mel King's Rainbow
           Coalition: Political Changes in
           Boston, 1963-1983
           James Green 99

VII	What's Black, White and Racist All Over?	
	William Alberts	137
VIII	Black Politics in America: From Access to Power	
	James Jennings	175

Index of Names 193

Contributors

James Jennings is Associate Professor of Political Science and Dean of the College of Public and Community Service, University of Massachusetts at Boston. He has written extensively on black and Puerto Rican politics in urban America. He is co-author of *Puerto Rican Politics in Urban America*.

Melvin H. King is Adjunct Professor and Director of the Community Fellows Program at Massachusetts Institute of Technology. He served in the Massachusetts State Legislature as Representative between 1973 and 1982. He campaigned for mayor of Boston in 1979 and 1983. In 1983, he became the first black mayoral candidate in the city's history to win the preliminary election and to run in the general election. He is the author of *Chain of Change*, a historical chronology of the struggle for black community development in Boston.

Hubert E. Jones is the Dean of the School of Social Work at Boston University. He ran for Congress in 1972, in the ninth congressional district. He is the founder of the Massachusetts Advocacy Center and has been a leading advocate for children's services and children's rights.

James Green is Professor of History at the College of Public and Community Service, University of Massachusetts at Boston. He has written extensively on the American labor movement. He is the author of *The World of the Worker* and *Grass-Roots Socialism*.

William E. Alberts is Minister of The Community Church of Boston, and a member of the Unitarian Universalist Association. His Ph.D. is from Boston University in the field of psychology and pastoral counseling. He has written numerous popular essays and articles on racism and politics in Boston, which have appeared in newspapers, magazines and journals.

Preface

This is a collection of essays on black political developments in the city of Boston, and on the national level. Most of the articles were written and published between 1979 and 1984, a critical period for understanding the city's political arena for years to come. The major purpose of this book is to provide information, data and analysis about black political participation in Boston. Collectively, the essays also place developments in Boston within a national context.

The collection examines the political history and development of blacks in Boston from the turn of the twentieth century to the present. The authors help to redress the prevalent notion that black politics is somehow a post-World War II phenomenon in this city. The political behavior patterns of blacks in Boston are also examined. These essays generate discussion of black politics in Boston and urban America in ways which have not been possible before, due to the casual and often inaccurate information about blacks provided through the written and visual media.

Finally, this book is also a review and analysis of the Mel King mayoral campaigns. These two events represent a breakthrough in Boston's political terrain. Yet few have examined the significance of Mr. King's mayoral attempts. The city's leading political analysts, pundits and journalists have failed to study adequately the social and cultural dynamics which were part of the King campaigns. *From Access to Power* seeks to show the conceptual linkages between local electoral developments such as the Mel King for Mayor Campaigns in Boston, and events such as the Harold Washington victory in Chicago, and the Jesse Jackson presidential campaign.

After an overview by Hubert Jones of major black political developments in recent periods, a historical analysis is provided of black politics in Boston, from the turn of the century to the current period. The first chapter is based primarily on information appearing in two pre-WWII black newspapers, *The Boston Chronicle* and *The Guardian*. Also included in Part One is an essay analyzing the influence of socio-economic factors on black political participation and behavior patterns. The last essay of this section discusses the political relationship between blacks and city government during the Kevin White years (1967-1983).

Part Two examines the two Mel King for mayor campaigns in Boston. This section provides an essay discussing the "moral" orientation of both electoral campaigns. James Green discusses how the Mel King for mayor campaigns were organized, and also the issues and groups which reflected the direction of the two campaigns. William Alberts discusses the role that the media played.

The Conclusion, by James Jennings, is a commentary on how black politics has evolved in the last few years in Boston and on the national level. This nation is witnessing the growth of a black politics which has become increasingly more concerned with "power." This new politics is emerging from a politics previously based on "access." The difference between these two related terms is examined in various ways by the contributors.

"Urban Machinism and The Black Voter: The Kevin White Years" first appeared in *The New Black Vote*, edited by Rod Bush (Synthesis Publications, San Francisco, 1984). "Three Stages of Black Politics in Boston" is from Mel King, *Chain of Change* (South End Press, Boston, 1980). James Green's article, "The Making of the Rainbow Coalition" first appeared in *Radical America*, Volume 17, Number 6 (November/December, 1983). The article by William Albert was published by Community Change, Inc. (1984). "Race, Class and Politics in the Black Community of Boston," by James Jennings, was originally published in the *Review of Black Political Economy* (Fall, 1981). "Politics and Morality in Boston," by James Jennings and Melvin I. King, was part of a special issue of *Debate and Understanding* (Summer 1983).

* * * * * *

Thanks are extended to Ruth Avitia, Vivienne Simon and Debra Horne for editorial assistance in the organization and compilation of materials for this study. Thanks are also extended to Ed Beard and the John W. McCormack Institute of Public Affairs, University of Massachusetts at Boston for a grant to complete this book.

J.J.
M.K.

INTRODUCTION

by *Hubert E. Jones*

Politics for blacks in Boston has been an illusory search for power, but also an essential quest for dignity and self-development. Since before the turn of this century to the present day, blacks have pursued relentlessly the acquisition of political power. They have done this in spite of being a numerical minority living in a social, cultural and economic structure that is arrayed against black interests. The charting of the long tradition of black political activism in Boston by James Jennings and Melvin I. King destroys the myth of black political passivity that still holds currency in some quarters. Throughout the odyssey of black political development in Boston, blacks have continually grappled with strategic considerations about how to fashion black voters into a bloc vote capable of making the decisive difference, particularly in close elections. This quest for political clout has involved politicizing blacks to transcend allegiances to political parties, political clubs and social institutions in order to amass black voter strength for the viable black candidates for office, or for white candidates who were responsive to black interests and needs. Black Bostonians have consistently demonstrated political sophistication and flexibility, revealing the saliency of race over social class, by forsaking traditional political affiliations and by forming new alliances when the political interests of blacks are at stake. The modern motto, articulated by the Congressional Black Caucus, is: ". . . no permanent friends, no permanent enemies, just permanent interests." This has been the operational philosophy of black political actors from the early 1900s to the 1980s.

The history of black politics in Boston is the story of determination and resiliency in the face of overwhelming odds created by an electoral system fraught with racism. During every time period in this century, blacks ran for elective offices over and over again. After absorbing political defeats, black politicians regrouped and reformulated political alliances in new efforts to prevail against "insurmountable" numerical odds. This proud legacy of persistence and political logistics is the foundation upon which current black political activism now rests.

The cruelest form of racism experienced by the black community and its political leaders has been the failure of white officeholders to reward black voters adequately for making their political successes possible. Whether it was the gubernatorial election of Leverett Saltonstall in 1940 or the mayoral elections of Kevin White in the late 1960s and 1970s, white politicians have taken the black vote for granted by failing to include blacks in the governance of the state and city and by failing to deliver services and jobs sought by the black community. Even in the face of political reality, white politicians have manifested the psychological need to deny that their political successes were due in part to the black vote. In too many cases, blacks were unwilling or unable to punish white politicians who failed to recognize the political debt owed to black voters. Unfortunately, black politicians and community leaders were often co-opted by token reward systems and threats of political retribution if continued political support was not forthcoming. The political machinations of Mayor Kevin White in relation to black politics is a grand example of this phenomenon.

As Mel King reveals in his chapter, the dependence of black service institutions on public funds under the control of city hall served to erode an independent black political base capable of holding officeholders accountable in the late 1950s and 1960s. King terms this period "the service stage," because it focused on black's dependency on others. In Boston, the service stage embellished by federal anti-poverty funding coincided with a period of black political drought. That is, blacks were unsuccessful in obtaining seats on the Boston School Committee, and gained only one seat on the Boston City Council during this period. In the absence of elected political leadership, service institutions and their leaders served as "politicians" mediating between the black community and downtown resources. Consequently, the gatekeeper role traditionally assumed by politicians representing the black community was transferred to service institutions. These institutional "politicians" negotiated with white officeholders, foundations and corporate leaders concerning the flow and direction of resources into the black community. As a result, the black political electoral base was undermined as funding from various sources was utilized by external forces to create competing power centers. Citizen participation mechanisms were designed to allocate limited public funds and political fragmentation was fostered by a focus on the survival of service institutions dependent on these public funds. In the absence of elected leadership and because of a weakened political fabric, the competition for financial resources became the source of inter-organizational disputes and battles, with destructive consequences for the service institutions involved and black politics in general.

The vestiges of this developmental period remain. Even though the black community now has adequate elected representation at all levels of government, black institutional leaders are reluctant to give up the gatekeeper/broker role and transfer it back to elected politicians. This can most constructively occur within a political organizational framework to which institutional leaders and elected politicians give allegiance. To allow external actors to determine the brokers for the black community's interests, in the name of pluralism, is to thwart healthy black political development.

The eternal search for black political mechanisms to harness the black vote and direct it toward collective ends goes on. Currently, the Black Political Task Force, formed in 1978, is the most prominent vehicle utilized for this purpose. In a relatively short period of time, it has played an effective role in unifying political support for black candidates as well as for white ones. Its perceived clout is revealed by the number of candidates for office who submit to a review process in order to obtain the endorsement of the Black Political Task Force and access to its political organizing resources. The political power of the task force has been enhanced by the dramatic increase in black voter registration during 1982 and 1983. The mobilization of the black vote in behalf of Mel King's candidacy for mayor confirms that black bloc voting is a powerful weapon in pursuit of black interests. Consequently, black votes will be sought increasingly by candidates for all local city offices as well as major statewide offices. The Black Political Task Force must now meet its great opportunity to achieve political unification by securing the financial, technical and human resources required to operate a smoothly operating apparatus that can consistently deliver on election day. This is a point of danger as well as an opportunity for the black community and its political development. Powerful political mechanisms usually conjure up the scary image of a collective czar and a small clique controlling the political destiny of the black community. The other usual concern is that a powerful group of actors will merely pursue personal political gain. Hence, it is not unlikely that substantial community actors who perceive themselves to be outside of the power circle will make the case for pluralistic power bases. The challenge for the Black Political Task Force is to demonstrate a participatory inclusiveness that welcomes all factions in the black community to this crucial political development work. The openness of the task force's work and processes will hopefully counteract normal anxieties and resistances. It is on the threshold of an enormous breakthrough in contributing to black political power in Boston.

The passage of city charter reform that mandated district representation for the school committee and city council is a boon to black political development. Although many political observers fret about the possible return of narrow parochialism to Boston's politics, this major change has increased political representation in the black community and will help to build the black power base. The increased competition in predominantly black districts for elective office will substantially increase black voter registration and voting. Within five years or less, the black community's registration base could be large enough to guarantee the capture of city hall. The lesson of the 1983 mayoral campaign is that a sizeable black voter base is a pre-condition to an effective coalition with white progressive activists. The abandonment by white liberals of Mel King, black mayoral candidate, to support Ray Flynn revealed that they ultimately respect political muscle and black political leadership that is in concert with their professed politics and ideology. The racism expressed in this is sobering; without the critical voting bloc, black leadership in Boston cannot hope to shape a response to a political agenda which would meet the needs and interests of the poor and people of color and make that agenda prevail throughout the turbulence of the electoral process. The politics of inclusion are not possible without the politics of black power.

The sophistication of black politics must expand beyond the electoral arena. Important decisions about the allocation of resources and opportunities in the city are also made outside of the political arena where elected officials reign. The influence and clout of universities, corporations, media and cultural institutions operate in ways to determine how and to whom the city will develop and allocate its resources. This informal governance works in tandem with governmental decision-making. Because blacks in Boston do not have equal access to substantial positions in these institutions or comparable institutions of their own, they are excluded from this aspect of politics in Boston. For this reason, it is crucial that black institutions and political mechanisms develop means to network with blacks in influential positions in the private sector. The absence of systematic networking among black politicians and black opinion makers undermines the potential impact blacks can have on informal governance in the city.

Politics in any American city cannot be understood outside the context of the fear and anxiety that plagues the American people. Citizens can no longer ignore the reality that corporate America has sold them a bill of goods that is fraudulent. The collusion of corporations and government at all levels has allowed the toxic waste from manufacturing processes to poison the atmosphere, the rivers, the streams and drinking wells. Pesticides are being used by farmers and fruit growers that result in toxic food products. The causal relationship between exposure to toxins and ill health and death is no longer in dispute. Our political leaders have presented us with an "economy of scarcity," claiming that there are fewer jobs, resources and social utilities for the American people to share, leading to a no-win competition for what is available. Scarcity is marketed at the same time that billions of dollars are poured by our federal government into excessive military expenditures. Consequently, federal social programs desperately needed by the poor and the elderly are reduced or eliminated. In a nation where our political leaders believe that recession is more acceptable than inflation, our people now know that at least 7% unemployment is a "structural" economic reality for the foreseeable future. The expanding arms race, accompanied by foreign policy sabre rattling, contribute to a general fear that nuclear holocaust is now becoming more than possible.

This overall context has generated fear and anxiety in all Americans, which shapes their orientations and encounters with politics in our cities. The current political arrangements and the politicians that sustain and benefit from them are held in suspicion and distrust. At the same time, people want politics and government to work and make possible an equitable distribution of resources and protections.

Despite all of its faults and shortcomings, the political system still holds the allegiance of the people. At worst, the American people have a love-hate orientation toward politics. The hate emanates from rage over deplorable social and economic conditions that exist and that are getting worse. The love flows from the ingrained faith that the economic system and government will deliver on the American promise of prosperity, security and fairness.

The complexity of the love-hate phenomenon must be taken into account in efforts to build a new black politic. Like other Americans, blacks are aware of the great need for new political arrangements: party realignments, independent parties, participatory mechanisms, decentralized decision-making and protective devices to defend against corruption and discrimination. Unfortunately, the path to political transformation is obstructed by the cult of personality, which is promoted by the mass media. The positive side of the ambivalence regarding politics is manipulated to assure voters that the right person (candidate) who possesses the right competence and personal qualities will set government straight. In the case of big city politics, the cult of personality represses the knowledge that any big city mayor is merely a political manager beholden to the "metropolitan establishment," composed of banking, real estate, academic, commercial and media conglomerates whose interests and goals are divergent from those of the working class, the poor and people of color.

Therefore, the building of a progressive black politics in Boston, or in any city, must counteract political behavior that focuses on personality-oriented politics and traditional machine politics. At the heart of the new black politics must be an inclusive process that gives black voters access to any political mechanisms that are involved in the selection and endorsement of candidates for elective office. It must be a process that allows people of color to resolve political differences and allows them to avoid counter-productive competition for political seats. It must recognize that the Latino and Asian-American constituencies have a right to political representation and that black political power must support the candidacies of persons from these ethnic groups. Sharing political power, as a matter of fact, must be one of the moral bases of progressive black politics.

PART ONE
Race and Politics in Boston, 1900-1983

I
Black Politics in Boston 1900-1950

James Jennings

The belief that only until very recently the black community in Boston was apolitical has been prevalent for many years. It has been perpetuated by scholars, journalists and political pundits.

One writer, Ralph Otwell, described blacks in Boston in the early sixties as representing a "political paradox," because

> in no other major city has a Negro been the passive political force he has been in the Boston scene. It would appear that as he multiplied in numbers, he dwindled in political weight. Compare his political lethargy with his heritage, and the paradox is even more puzzling; for Boston was the cradle of abolition, the home of militant Negro agitation, the headquarters of an earlier political ferment.[1]

Echoing this a few years later, another observer noted:

> In looking at Boston one is greeted with a number of mixed and often contradictory impressions. The Negro in Boston is something of an anomaly. Few other black communities can boast such early origins as freed men. Yet the Negro's demonstrable political strength has been something less than the "guilded" appearance of his long history would lead one to believe.[2]

These statements reflected the state of black political activities in the 1950s and 1960s. But as this chapter and those that follow will illustrate, the observations do not reflect black political activity today, or in the first fifty years of the twentieth century. There has been a heightened sense of electoral activity among blacks in Boston, especially after the two Mel King mayoral campaigns in 1979 and 1983. This heightened electoral activism is not new for blacks in Boston. Between the early 1900s and late 1940s, there were numerous attempts by blacks to gain electoral representation. The focus of this activity was access to patronage controlled by city government. In the 1980s, however, while blacks do seek political access through electoral activism, there are at least two new developments. First of all, blacks are moving from a focus on access to a focus on power. The differences between electoral activism based on seeking access and the pursuit of power will be explained in subsequent chapters. In addition to this, sectors which did not pursue electoral activity previously in Boston's history, are now beginning to do so. The purpose of this chapter is to describe and analyze black electoral activity between 1900 and 1950.

Despite its small size the black community exhibited a relatively high degree of electoral activism and political sophistication before WWII. In the early 1900s John Daniels explained how the black vote was used in ways which selectively rewarded friends and punished ingrates.[3] In 1901, for example, Boston's Ward 18, a bastion of black Republican voters, supported the Democratic nominee for mayor because of dissatisfaction with the Republicans. And again, in spite of a strongly entrenched tradition of voting Republican, black voters in Boston supported John H. Fitzgerald, the Democratic nominee for mayor in 1905 and 1907, due to his 'pro-Negro' statements in Congress.

In 1909, after supporting the Republican candidate for the position of district attorney in previous elections, the black community threw its support to the Democratic candidate. This was done because the white Republican district attorney (Arthur D. Hill) removed James G. Wolff, a black, from a clerkship in the district attorney's office.

In the early and mid-1900s, leaders such as William Monroe Trotter encouraged black voters to give their support to those candidates who promised the most to blacks. John Daniels offers insights to Trotter's political leadership:

> If Negroes voted in an independent bloc, Trotter argued, they could swing close elections in their favor and then make demands on the men they elected. 'The Negro holds the balance of power in several of the Northern states,' the Guardian would announce; or again, '... according to a well calculated estimate, the colored race can decide the congressional election this fall... We can yet save ourselves by a judicious placing of our ballot.'[4]

Black voters during this period organized themselves into a political force that could not be ignored:

As contrasted with their former political dependence on the Whites, and their rather slavish following of the Republican Party, the Negroes are at present drawing together among themselves as a self-reliant racial group, and have already in considerable measure brought their independent political leverage to bear in the protection and advancement of their own collective welfare. As the combined result of their progress in these several respects, they have succeeded in making themselves a reckonable factor in the body politics and in obtaining substantial political recognition in the form of an increasing number of appointments to public positions of trust and credit.[5]

Black citizens continued to use their few votes effectively in later years.

Since black voters could not be ignored electorally, they were constantly appealed to by white politicians for support. Writing in the early 1940s, David Jordan found that:

Since there is little of machine politics in Boston, the minority groups received great amounts of attention from candidates for office, officeholders seeking re-election or advance to higher political office, in those elections where the popular vote determines who shall fill the position. Thus, the Negro group finds itself an integral part of the voting population of Boston.[6]

In this same study, Jordan interviewed James Michael Curley in the Spring of 1942. Curley stated to Jordan that

The Negro vote is important in Boston in city elections, there are 20,000 registered voters, who today vote the Democratic ticket. Invariably, elections are settled by less than 10,000 votes. So, in a sense, they have the balance of power...

The prospects of Negroes acquiring political power in Boston which they now possess, are excellent, since they have acquired a knowledge of their power and the necessity of unified action.[7]

Jordan arrived at the following conclusion in his study of black political development in pre-WWII Boston:

Even without electing a Negro, the power of a unified Negro vote would necessitate consideration of demands made by the colored people. For the Negroes could hold the balance of power in all close elections and could make any election so close that they could constitute a serious threat to any and all candidates for office.

Although there were no successful candidates for the few elected offices available to blacks between the two World Wars, black citizens were represented by strong political leaders whose influence was based on black voter turnout. According to various descriptions appearing in the *Boston Chronicle* and *The Guardian*, black leadership was pluralistic: a myriad of organizations provided input in deciding the electoral direction of the black community between the early 1900s and the late 1940s. This is reflected in the community meetings and forums that were called frequently for citizens in the predominantly black wards. In Ward 4 and Ward 9, there were numerous popular and actively-supported Democratic and Republican clubs.

The issues which blacks emphasized remained uniform during this period. The political platforms of black candidates usually included demands for better housing, more recreational facilities and park space for black citizens, better governmental representation of black interests, more and better street-lighting fixtures and paving in black neighborhoods, and finally, judicial, civic and political appointments of blacks. The Reverend S.M. Riley, Jr. of the Fourth Methodist Church summarized the kinds of benefits which blacks in Roxbury and the South End hoped to obtain from local political activity. At the fourth anniversary dinner (1942) of the Greater Boston Negro Trade Association, which was founded under the auspices of the Phi Beta Sigma Fraternity, the Reverend stated that blacks should seek the following rewards for their ballot box activities:

1. playground facilities
2. protection for pedestrians and children
3. the removal of electrical wires from over the tennis courts at the William E. Carter playground
4. the re-opening of the branch library in Ward 9
5. better housing
6. jobs

During this period, there were political splits in the black community between Republicans, Democrats and Independents. In many instances, however, these splits were resolved by black leaders to avoid diluting the black vote. Many elections saw black political activists overcome their differences in order to support one black candidate. In 1938, for example, black Democrats split in Roxbury, and two candidacies were announced for the state representative race. Shag Taylor was slated by the Colored Democratic Club, and Joseph Nelson was endorsed by the Eastern New England Congress, a civil rights group. Ultimately, in the interest of racial unity, the influential Shag Taylor announced his withdrawal from the race and endorsed Nelson. The Republicans supported Alfred Houghton against Joseph Nelson. Both Houghton and Nelson survived their respective primaries in September of that year. Both men campaigned on seeing a black man become the first state representative in Massachusetts; the loser would support the winner. In the same year, black voters helped to nominate Curley as the Democratic gubernatorial candidate. Under Shag Taylor's influence, the black community supported Curley, six to one. Martin P. Richardson, writing for the *Boston Chronicle*, saw this period as signalling something new and positive in the political development of the black community. After the primary election, he wrote:

> The record registration, the intense activity of colored workers at the booths—and much of it was free-will work, at that—and the heavy vote showed a healthful trend forward, full participation in political affairs rather than the old apathy and laxity of past years.

He continued:

> The rejection of the honeyed promises from the sheriff's office indicates a sort of political emancipation not far different from the unchaining for which Abraham Lincoln became famous 75 years ago. It provided an active proof that mere promises can no longer fool the colored voter. It served notice on all politically "hopeful" (sic) that campaign promises will have to in the future, be followed by a certain amount of fair and proportionate consideration.[8]

Although Curley lost this election to Saltonstall, and all the black candidates also lost, voters in the black community provided a respectable showing for the black candidates.

The growing activism of the black voter was not overlooked by white politicians and government officials of the day. As a response to agitation in the South End and Roxbury, Harry A. Loftin, a black man and an officer of the Roxbury Court, was appointed probation officer in February, 1940. This appointment was a result of a recommendation made by black political activists. Hubert Clarke, another black citizen, was selected to take the place of Loftin as the court officer of the Roxbury Court. White politicians at the local and state levels approached seriously the black voter. Councilor Daniel Sullivan, who defeated David A. Kenny by only four hundred votes out of more than seven thousand cast in the 1939 race, promised the black residents of Roxbury better services than they had been receiving.

The door appeared to have opened a little wider as a result of growing black electoral activism. Shag Taylor's influence at the local and state levels was recognized and highly respected by this time. He was selected as a delegate to the National Convention of the Democratic Party in 1940. A few months later, the state Democratic Convention chose him as a presidential elector. Another emerging powerful individual from the black community during this period, Ralph "Fats" Johnson, was appointed as Secretary to the Democratic Committee of Ward 9 (1940), about a month after he won election to this then-influential body.

The growing influence and sophistication of the black community is evidenced at the state level in the gubernatorial election of 1940. Although President Roosevelt carried the black vote in Massachusetts, Leverett Saltonstall, the Republican candidate for governor, received the bulk of the black vote. As a result of this, Saltonstall won the election. As reported by the *Boston Chronicle*, Saltonstall won by nine thousand votes; he attracted about ten thousand black votes. Blacks provided the governor with his margin of victory. At the local level, the black citizens of Roxbury and the South End were determined by this time to elect one of their own to either the city council or the state legislature. A long series of defeats over the course of thirty years were not enough to deter them from continuing their efforts. In the summer of 1940, three black citizens filed nomination papers for the state representative race in Ward 9. William S. Sparrow and Lawrence Banks filed as Republicans, and Dr. Irving Gray filed as a Democrat. In the 1941 city council primary race, three black candidates found themselves bidding for a seat: Lawrence Banks, David Kenny and Simeon Roberts. Before the general election, Banks and Roberts aligned themselves with Kenny. He was again defeated, however, by David Sullivan, the white incumbent.

In the following year (1942), two black candidates vied for the Republican Party nomination for state representative in Ward 9. Lawrence Banks beat Maurice Smith in the primary battle and became the sole black candidate in the general election. He lost to a white candidate, Dennis Glynn of the Democratic Party, by only 319 votes. Banks ran again in 1944 and again lost to Glynn in the general election by a few votes. In the Democratic Party Primary for this election, Glynn defeated another black candidate, Roy Teixeira (1,362 to 716 votes). In 1945, Banks ran for the city council seat of Ward 9 and lost by six hundred (600) votes; however, he won all the black precincts of Roxbury. Finally, in 1946, there were three early black candidates for the state representative seat. In the interest of racial solidarity, David Kenny and John McIlviane dropped out to support Lawrence Banks for the Ward seat. At the same time, William E. Harrison became the black candidate for the seat in Ward 12. Despite a strong 3,000 vote showing by Harrison, he lost. But for the first time in the twentieth century, a black man was elected to the state legislature; Lawrence Banks became the state representative for Ward 9 in Roxbury. Banks beat Dennis Glynn, who had defeated him in the Democratic Party primary by 4,753 to 3,900 votes. This helped mobilize the black community further, and in 1947, Maurice L. Smith, while losing to the popular white incumbent David Sullivan in the city council race, won every black precinct in Ward 9; even though he lost by seven hundreds votes, the black candidate won all the black precincts.

After serving two years as state representative, Lawrence Banks was defeated in the general state election of 1948 after winning the Republican Party nomination. He lost to Glynn in the Democratic Party primary by only nineteen (19) votes. In the general election, Glynn beat the incumbent, 6,037 to 5,151 votes; Banks carried all the black precincts in this election. This did not deter Banks from pursuing other electoral offices. In 1949, he ran against Sullivan for the Ward 9 City Council seat, and lost by a mere six (6) votes (4,377 to 4,371). The election was appealed on the basis of voting irregularities; as a consequence, Sullivan was seated until August 1951, while Banks was unable to replace him until after that time. While this issue was being settled in the courts, Banks also attempted to unseat Glynn as the state representative after having defeated Glynn in the Republican Party primary (Glynn, however, defeated Banks in the Democratic Party primary). In the general state election of 1950, Glynn beat Banks, 6,409 to 3,617 votes. After 1950, Lawrence Banks continued to pursue electoral office. He lost in 1952 in the state representative race and also lost in 1954; for both races, he was the Republican Party nominee.

Despite the small size of the black community before the 1950s, then, electoral activity was pursued actively. While some black leaders concentrated on protest activities usually revolving around national and international racial issues, other black leaders focused their attention on the local electoral arena. Individuals like Shag Taylor, Robert Merritt, Mabel Worthy and Lawrence Banks were able to deliver black votes and sponsor black candidacies for state and city elections in Ward 9 and Ward 12. The returns which black leaders in the electoral arena sought to obtain were the traditional kinds of rewards. These included petty patronage and favors from city hall and the governor, as well as civic appointments.

It seems that some sectors in the black community did not tend to follow black party leaders and activists such as Shag Taylor and his ilk into local politics as readily as did other black citizens. Many not involved in electoral activism were engaged in other kinds of political activism. Between the 1900s and 1940s, there were protest activities organized around such issues as the showing of racist films ("Birth of a Nation" and Walt Disney's production, "The Song of the South"), school issues, desegregation of various public places, and unemployment.[9]

Under the leadership of people like Lillian Williams in the mid-1930s, some blacks became involved in various protest activities outside the electoral arena. They staged marches for jobs, picketed stores and conducted voter registration drives. Edith Washington, Director of the Youth Council of the NAACP, led a campaign in the late 1930s to urge businesses operating in black neighborhoods to employ black residents from those areas. The New England Congress for Equal Opportunities spearheaded a strong anti-lynching campaign. Other groups, like the Theta Alpha Chapter of the Zeta Phi Beta Sorority and the Phi Beta Sigma and Beta Alpha Chapters of the Phi Beta Sigma Fraternity, concentrated on national issues also. In Boston, the "cosmopolitan" blacks or those blacks who concentrated on national and systemic issues provided a basis for the growth of the NAACP.

In conclusion, the relatively small black community was politically active. It also was sophisticated, judging by its protest activities, its swing-vote history and "bloc" behavior in the electoral arena. Although it operated within a context of segregation, the black community was aggressive in seeking elected offices. A second conclusion, which remains tentative until harder evidence is uncovered, is that there seems to have developed in black Boston two general political orientations.[11] One, which seems to have attracted those blacks with more cosmopolitan outlooks, focused on national issues or local issues which affected social relations between blacks and whites in Boston. This orientation encouraged protest-type activities that could touch any area of black-white interaction. The other orientation was contained in the city's electoral arena. This style of orientation was exhibited by Shag Taylor and Robert Merritt, political bosses of Roxbury and the South End. This same orientation focused on the development of political influence for the purpose of patronage. To use Dahl's classic terms, the latter orientation sought divisible benefits for the black community, but the former primarily focused on indivisible benefits.[12] Those seeking divisible benefits utilized electoral politics, while the others sought this through other channels. To a certain degree, these orientations were reflected in the two black newspapers produced in Boston, *The Guardian* and *The Boston Chronicle*. The former seems to have adopted a more national outlook than the latter; *The Boston Chronicle* seems to have devoted greater coverage to local political developments.[13]

There is some evidence to show that in the past, these political views came into conflict, although not to the degree that Wilson and Banfield described in their studies of Chicago's black community.[14] Instances of this conflict included attempts to establish "colored" Democratic Clubs and organizations in the 1920s and 30s.[15] Some integrationists were against these attempts, because they supposedly encouraged segregationist practices. But for the most part, these orientations do not seem to have produced any long standing 'hard split'; at times, the differences were not very clear-cut. These differences were probably reflections of the composition of the black community.

The two black major political orientations were adopted by different social sectors of the black community. Byron Rushing, president of the Museum of Afro-American History, has described the three major black social groupings in Boston before WWII: black citizens of West Indian descent, black citizens who migrated from the South, and what Rushing refers to as "... those who think of themselves as 'Black Bostonians.'"[16] A number of studies and commentaries suggest that those who might be considered "Black Bostonians" have not been inclined to 'roll up their sleeves' and become involved in the intricacies of local electoral politics. Adelaide Hill stated that the upper-class black citizens concentrated more on social issues within the group rather than on politics. If the "Black Bostonian" element sought political involvement, it was usually at the national level, rather than at the local and state levels. They tended to be concerned with broad black and white social and civic relations and national race issues. This led them to the NAACP and the Urban League and to the kinds of activities sponsored by these organizations. A review of the topics and editorials of *The Boston Chronicle* suggest that the West Indian sector was attracted to both kinds of political orientations. One could not accurately argue that this group was attached to one kind of orientation at the expense of the other. West Indian Blacks were involved in protest activities, associated with the NAACP and the Urban League, but they were also part of efforts to institutionalize black politics in the local electoral arena.

Blacks from the South may have been more attracted to local electoral politics than to the national protest organizations. It was probably easier for Southern black citizens to find a welcome in this type of politics than in those arenas controlled by established "Black Bostonians," including the West Indians. There is some evidence, although slight, that suggests that the black citizens from the South were at times resented by the other two segments. Evidence of this can be found in some of the editorials of *The Boston Chronicle* in the 1920s and 1930s. In criticizing the political passivity of some sectors in the black community before WWII, Jordan blamed the blacks who were Southern-born or of Southern parentage, thus:

> ...As most of the Negroes in Boston are either southern-born or of southern parentage, many of them are greatly influenced by southern practices, customs and traditions. This means that most of the colored, falling in this category, possess an inferiority complex, and a feeling of humbleness and servility.[17]

And, much earlier, Daniels argued that the passivity of Southern blacks kept this sector from gaining acceptance by the other black groups in Boston. He wrote:

> ...The great majority of immigrants from the South, no less because of their own ignorance and lack of interest in political affairs than because of their previous exclusion from politics by the Southern whites, have acquired next to no political experience and understanding. Even after taking up their abode in Boston, they tend, through their own inertia, to remain in a benighted state.[18]

If there ever was such a thing as resentment against the Southern black, it seems to have disappeared by the 1950s and 1960s. Today, it is not possible to distinguish these particular groups in terms of their political orientations. Blacks with West Indian backgrounds and those of Southern descent can be found to be equally involved with electoral politics.

The political activism in the electoral arena evidenced in the black community before WWII seems to have halted, or at least slowed considerably since the end of the 1940s. The 1950s witnessed a lull in black electoral activism; the black community was beginning to use other channels to seek satisfaction of its wants. Melvin I. King refers to the 1950s as the "Service Stage" of the black community's evolution since WWII to the present. He characterizes this period as one which highlights the dependency of blacks upon the white society:

> ... The Service Stage, a period roughly covering the 1940s, 50s and very early 60s, was a time during which the community of color was dependent on the "goodwill" of the white society for access to its goods, its services, its jobs, housing and schools. The dependency was based on the primarily negative self-image of black people and the external control of resources and institutions in the black community which kept black people subservient.[19]

This development was partially due to the increasing number of black citizens migrating into Boston. The 1950s became a transitional period which linked the "old" black community with the "new" one. The demographic dislocations which occurred interrupted the development of black electoral progress.

Notes

1. Ralph Otwell, "The Negro in Boston", in Edward C. Banfield and Martha Derthick *A Report on the Politics of Boston Massachusetts*, Joint Center for Urban Studies, Cambridge, Ma., 1960, p. 45.
2. Charles J. Hamilton, Jr. "Changing Patterns of Negro Leadership in Boston", doctoral dissertation, Harvard University, 1969, p. 15.
3. John Daniels, *In Freedom's Birthplace*, Arno Press, New York, 1914, 1969, Chapter entitled "The Leverage of the Ballot."
4. Stephen Fox, *The Guardian of Boston*, Atheneum, New York, 1970, p. 147.
5. Daniels, *op. cit.*, p. 307.
6. Oswald Jordan, "The Political Status of the Negro in Boston," Masters essay, Howard University, 1942, p. 17.
7. *Ibid.*, p. 21
8. *The Boston Chronicle*, September 24, 1938.

9. Fox, *op. cit.*, Chapter entitled: "After 1919: You Don't Understand, You See One Side, the Public Another Side, But I See the Third Side."

11. Edward C. Banfield and Martha Derthick suggest that these political orientations were also found in a later period. See *A Report on the Politics of Boston, Massachusetts*, Joint Center for Urban Studies, Cambridge, MA., 1960, p. 72.

12. Robert Dahl, *Who Governs*, Yale University Press, New Haven, CT., 1960.

13. This dichotomy developed in other cities too; however, the particular form which it took depended on the social context of the city. Kusmer found that, in Cleveland,

> ... Among some of the older leaders of the black community who had pinned their hopes on an integrated society, there was a mounting sense of despair over the rising tide of racism and the consolidation of the ghetto. The new group of rising black businessmen, politicians and professionals who relied predominantly on black patronage for their livelihoods greeted these trends with more equanimity. Although somewhat disturbed over discrimination, this newer leadership group— especially the businessmen—viewed the ghetto chiefly in positive terms, seeing in it a clear justification for their philosophy of racial solidarity and self-help.

See Kenneth L. Kusmer, A Ghetto Takes Shape: Black Cleveland, 1870-1930, University of Illinois Press, Chicago, 1976, p. 235.

14. James Q. Wilson, *Negro Politics: The Search for Leadership*, The Free Press, Glencoe, IL, 1960, and Edward Banfield *Political Influence*, The Free Press, Glencoe, IL, 1961.

15. Fox, *op. cit.*, pps. 263-266; also, see Jordan, p. 92.

16. Interview with Byron Rushing, July 17, 1980.

17. Jordan, *op. cit.*, p. 59

18. Daniels, *op. cit.*, p. 277

19. Melvin I. King, *Chain of Change*, South End Press, Boston, MA, 1981, p. 4.

II

Three Stages of Black Politics in Boston, 1950-1980

Mel King

My theory about the stages of black community development has evolved out of my experience with the process of change in Boston's black community over the past thirty years. The theory is built around a chronological framework, although it is important to realize that the stages of development did not occur at exactly the same time in the different areas of development which will be described in this book: education, housing, politics, and economic development. No evolutionary process is completely smooth; at times events in the community appear to double back on themselves, overlap or reiterate one another. But the theory provides an outline for what appears to me to be the major direction and types of change for our community over the past several decades.

The three stages are the service stage, the organizing stage, and the institution building stage. In the course of these stages, there have been accompanying psychological changes, as the self-image of people of color evolved from negative to positive, from dependence to independence. A similar evolution has marked the power relationships shaping community change. During the period of negative self-image the community was essentially powerless. As the community has moved toward a more positive self-image, its power has increased and it has gained control over more of its own affairs and has begun to demand accountability in terms of both political and economic power relationships. At the same time, one of the most important products of this change process has been the skills which people have acquired. The black community is acquiring the skills to be able to lead itself and others. Struggle has proven to be one of the most effective means of education; and the acquisition of skills has supported the positive changes in self-image and has contributed to the building of power in the community.

Chronologically, the stages have roughly corresponded to the decades of the fifties, sixties and seventies, with some significant overlap. The fifties and early sixties were the period of the service stage, of being dependent. During that time we fought to have access to the services available to others in the society, pressing to be allowed to vote, to eat and drink where we wanted, to be able to use public facilities, hotels, motels, parks and other resources which had been denied to people of color for generations. The efforts to get jobs, decent education and other basic American opportunities were all focused on the services offered by churches, social service agencies, settlement houses, charity groups and "concerned" business and commercial groups. We did not see clearly the dependence and debilitation which a service relationship creates. We did not understand that as long as we waited for others to help us, we would never be able to take charge of our own lives. We always assumed that our inability to get access was due to our own inadequacies; our schools weren't as good, so our skills were not up to standard, our incomes didn't allow us to get decent housing, and our family life was inadequate. We did not understand for instance that in many cases it was not our children who were inadequate, but the deliberate segregative and discriminatory policies of the Boston School Committee which kept black youngsters from achieving excellence.

During the middle sixties we began to organize. We began to see ourselves differently. In this organizing stage, we understood that not only are we *deserving* of services in our own right as members of this society, but we are also *capable* of serving ourselves on our own terms. We were essentially powerless during the service stage, but as we moved into the organizing stage we began to assume some power in the process of working together to make institutions more responsive. Our collective voice began to be heard more clearly than our timid individual pleas for entry, and the political implications of working together began to be obvious.

In the late sixties, with the failure of the federal government's pretenses at building a "Great Society" and the timely diversion of energy from civil rights struggles to the Viet Nam war, not to mention the systematic murder of the leaders of the Civil Rights Movement, the community of color began to build its own institutions. Demanding access to existing institutions naturally led us to think about what we were trying to get into. Did we really want our children to be taught like the average white child in Boston? Did we want to build housing in ways that would require us to exploit others as we had been exploited? We began to understand that the society as it stands will never meet our needs on our terms because our terms are contradictory to many of its basic premises. So we began to develop our own institutions. Some of them were black versions of the societal norms; but many of them were genuine alternatives. Beyond just getting our share, we were working to change the quality and character of our share. During this period, the transformation of the black self-image became more dramatic. "Black Power" was a slogan which electrified black communities across the country, and we began to explore our heritage in earnest. We began to redefine blackness, to see its inherent beauty and worth, to understand its strength. We permanently changed the American language; we changed the way we dressed; we changed our self-image and the way others viewed us. And we built models which other groups have used.

The institution building stage began in the late sixties and extended throughout the seventies, a period in which increasing numbers of community groups in the black community formed to provide services or to carry out development plans for the black community. However, with the serious economic pressures brought by the Nixon administration's policies in housing and education, and the oil and energy crisis, inflation and a general recession, many of these fledgling institutions perished for lack of resources; others retreated to an isolated course of self-preservation which has prevented much interaction with other kindred efforts. At the same time, during the seventies, "institutionalization" of many of our concerns was taking place in a variety of ways as existing structures had to accommodate some of our demands.

Most importantly, the late seventies were a time when we began to make links with other groups. Our consciousness and perspective broadened and led us to recognize the importance of forging links with groups engaged in struggles qualitatively similar to our own. We were determined to offer mutual support and protection during the battles ahead to preserve the gains we had made and to insist on further changes as we continued to struggle to transform our city. The result of these three stages is the community development process: the empowerment of people of color. If we can get all the community agencies and institutions working together to provide services directly to the community on our own terms, if we can humanize the political process street by street on a day to day basis and build organizing into our work as an ongoing process, we will have the basis of community development that will meet basic human needs.

All of the stages discussed have been the steps toward the process of community development which will integrate our lives in all the possible human and political dimensions—individual, family, community, city-wide, state, national, global, universal. As we move further into the experience of building coalitions and more deeply into the process of community (self) development, we will become increasingly powerful and increasingly positive in our view of ourselves and in our ability to lead and work with others. Our experience in the last thirty (or three hundred) years has provided the basis for our visions about what sort of city and society we need to make it all happen. We are ready to use power to build for our future.

THE INSTITUTION BUILDING STAGE

Beginning in 1971, there were a series of attempts to bring community and electoral organizing together, to hold black candidates accountable to the black community through an on-going black political organization. The first attempt was the calling of the "Bostown" Political Convention in August, 1971.

> For the first time in the history of Massachusetts politics, the Black community of "Boston" will come together to select its own candidates for public office. Through the mechanism of an independent Black political convention we are seeking to unify the Black community around the issues which the community deems most relevant. The nomination of candidates by Black community residents will be an unprecedented event in Boston Politics. —*Press Release*

The convention endorsed several candidates (including Tom Atkins for mayor), adopted a platform, and began a voter registration campaign.

The following spring, thirty-seven Massachusetts delegates attended the first national black political convention in Gary, Indiana. The delegates ratified a black agenda, dealing with the use of busing to gain quality education, the role of Israel in the Middle East, and the inauguration of a "National Assembly." As a result of this convention, the Massachusetts delegates set up the Massachusetts Black Political Assembly agenda, agreed upon in Gary, and took an oath to fight for resolution of these issues if elected to office.

On April 15, 1972 there was an "Action Caucus 72," a political convention of people of color, to endorse a candidate for U.S. Representative to run against Louise Day Hicks. The community endorsed Hubie Jones. Though Jones did not win, Hicks was defeated by John Moakley, a democrat, who ran as an independent. One of the problems behind the Jones candidacy was that despite the community endorsement for him, Mel Miller, owner of the *Bay State Banner*, a community based weekly newspaper, ran against Jones. The resulting competition between the two turned into a bitter fight based on personalities. This led us to abandon the development of a process by which we could seriously look at the options and make some decisions based on the importance of developing leadership to provide a cooperative approach to what Hubie Jones focused on (i.e. issues of concern to the community). Mel Miller spent his time trying to discredit Jones, rather than running a campaign to expose issues and propose solutions. Hubie Jones won the community aspect of the election, because people understood that Miller wasn't a serious candidate who was ready to deal with the real needs of the black community.

These three attempts to establish accountability from black elected officials came to fruition in 1972, with the establishment of the Massachusetts Black Caucus. As a result of redistricting in 1971, five black representatives were elected to the House in 1972—Doris Bunte, Bill Owens, Royal Bolling, Sr., Royal Bolling, Jr., and myself. After the election, members of the caucus met with David Bartley, the Speaker of the House, who agreed to provide us with a staff person. The five of us realized that we had to combine our resources in an effort to meet the needs of the black community. We agreed that the purpose of the caucus was:

> ... to work toward black empowerment across the State of Massachusetts ... and the caucus also understands that part of the reason for the black community's long-standing disempowerment is the ethnocentricity which exists in the system. It does not plan to perpetuate that behavior but rather to end it by seeking to build bridges with all people who believe that the system ought to operate in a pluralistic fashion to relate to them.

The black caucus was the real beginning of institution building in the electoral process. It was the first black political organization which sought to connect community and electoral organization on an ongoing basis. On New Years Day 1972, hosted by the Elma Lewis School, the five black state representatives held their first joint inaugural. It was phenomenal. The five of us took the following pledge:

> As a member of the Massachusetts Black Caucus, I pledge that I will conduct the daily affairs and decision making of my activity, and/or office, so as to reflect the actual, explicit desires and concerns of the Black Community beyond question. In this manner I will constantly act out of my accountability to the manifest interests of the Black Community.

This was the culmination and the beginning of all that we had been striving for since Ruth Batson's attempt to get elected to the school committee in 1959. Black elected officials were united together with the community to raise a unified voice for the need for black community development through community control.

One of the first major efforts of the caucus was to focus on police/community relations. Each of the representatives held meetings in their districts to discuss both police violence and police protection. After that we brought all the districts together. Fifteen hundred people came. The results: the caucus was given a community mandate to go to the city with a series of proposals dealing with crime analysis, police training, police monitoring, and community security patrols. However, when we met with Police Commissioner Robert DiGrazia, we ran into a stone wall. We got nothing out of DiGrazia. As a result, police/community relations have continued to deteriorate.

The major accomplishment of the caucus in the first two years was legislating a black senatorial seat through redistricting. In Boston, the major black wards were grouped with strong Irish and Jewish wards. As a result, there had never been a black senator in Massachusetts. In response to this lack of representation, there was a court order, in 1973, to redistrict the senatorial districts. The first two redistricting plans proposed by the senate would not have significantly affected the chance of electing a black senator, and were blocked by the black caucus. A third plan, which the caucus helped to draft, included a black district. Staff members Kay Gibbs and Dianne Renfro researched and organized the effort.

In 1973 the third redistricting plan was ratified. There was one unexpected vote by John Loring (R) Acton, Mass. Rep. Loring was contacted by a constituent, who asked that he not vote for a redistricting plan, unless provisions were made for a black senator. This contact helped to shape his decision; prior to that time he had not made up his mind (voters *can* impact the decision-making process of their elected officials).

The new senate seat, however, led to new problems in the black community. The election for the new seat led to a bitter contest between Bill Owens and Royal Bolling, Sr. Bill Owens, on the one hand, represented the younger generation of black politicians. He was in the National Black Political Assembly, and other black elected official organizations. Royal Bolling, Sr., on the other hand, was the senior member of the black caucus, and had fought hard for redistricting. He was an independent who had built his political career with his own hands over the years.

Bill Owens won the seat in the November election, and on New Years of 1975, he held his own separate inaugural before other incumbent representatives held their celebration at the Elma Lewis School. The conflict between Owens and Bolling not only split the community, but seriously weakened the caucus as well. As in the Jones and Miller contest in 1972, the campaigns were not fought on the basis of the issues, but deteriorated into personal politics taking precedence over the needs of the community.

This conflict between building personal power, as opposed to empowering the community, served to weaken the caucus and to weaken its relationship with the community. This was manifested by the breakdown in the attempts to work on police issues. Some black elected officials thought that the demands being made by the community would have a negative effect on their electability—that the demands of the community would be too radical. These officials felt that the more radical demands of the black community would jeopardize their support by the more conservative black middle class. But how could any black official be "too radical" given the oppression confronting the great majority of black people in Boston? Finally the result of this split was to retard our attempts to form an independent political organization.

CHARTER REFORM

In Boston, the school committee is made up of five members, and the city council is made up of nine city councilors. Both elections are at-large elections where people from all over the city vote for all candidates, and those candidates receiving the five, or nine, highest number of votes get elected. This type of an election favors those groups which have the largest voting block(s), and in this case whites, particularly the Irish from South Boston and West Roxbury. Also, in this type of election the number of seats available determines who gets represented. The fewer seats, say in the case of the school committee, makes it even more difficult for smaller neighborhoods, or for people of color in Boston, to be represented. This is gerrymandering by numbers, not by political boundaries. In addition, at-large elections favor candidates who have more money to spend on city-wide campaigns for advertising, campaign workers, etc. This makes it possible for the Brahmins in Boston and the organized public worker groups to put their support behind those candidates which are most supportive of their interests. An at-large election allows those with the largest demographic block or those with the most money to centralize control over the city. As a result, the black community has continually failed to gain representation on the city council and the school committee. The same is true for Allston/Brighton, Mission Hill, Jamaica Plain, and many of Boston's smaller ethnic neighborhoods.

In the November 1974 election, there was referendum question #7 (Charter Reform #1), which called for the abolition of the school committee and the appointment of the school superintendent by the mayor. This proposal was Major White's attempt to co-opt the movement to gain greater representation on the school committee by the black community and other ethnic groups without representation within the city.

Appropriately enough, the main opponents of question #7 were the anti-busing organizations, ROAR, the South Boston Information Center and the East Boston Information Center, who saw the referendum as a threat to their control over the school committee, and their ability to prevent busing and to dole out patronage. The referendum was defeated.

In August of 1975 the black community, led by Attorney Margaret

Burnham, went to the United States District Court claiming that, "the at-large system effectively cancels out, dilutes and minimizes the voting strength of the Boston black community in school committee elections."[1] The Court ruled against the claim that the at-large system was unconstitutional, attributing the lack of black representation primarily to low black voter registration and participation. Similarly, the judge's position was that Italians and other minorities had succeeded in getting representation and therefore if black folks would get out and vote they too could have representation. Once again, the problem was projected as black people, not an exclusionary system which had repeatedly defeated black efforts to change it.

After Mayor White was reelected in November 1975, he established the Committee for Boston which held a series of meetings, inviting community residents to discuss issues confronting them and possible solutions. A recommendation made by the committee was that the escalating violence in Boston could be alleviated by decentralizing power through charter reform based on district elections. However, Mayor White instead filed legislation to make the school committee a department of city government under the control of the city council. The state representatives from Boston were able to defeat the measure in the legislative committee of local affairs.

Two years later in the 1977 election the issue of neighborhood representation resurfaced in a referendum known as the "Galvin Plan." The Galvin Plan called for reorganization of both the school committee and the city council. Both would have nine district and four at-large representatives. Significantly, Mayor White did not support the plan, and it was opposed by the folks from South Boston and Charlestown. Despite the racism of those who are opposed to representation of people of color and to democratic participation of Boston neighborhoods, the Galvin Plan only lost by 3800 votes. The near approval of the Galvin Plan was the closest we have yet come to ending city imperialism—where people from one community decide what goes on in other communities, and take resources from those communities for their own development. That kind of imperialism is not any different from those policies pursued and determined by the United States government to exploit the resources of people of color in Africa, Asia and South America.

However, black attempts to be represented on the school committee finally met with success. Back in the November 1975 elections, John O'Bryant ran for school committee. An anti-busing newspaper distributed in South Boston prior to the election read:

> Well, wake up Southie. Do you realize you gave 834 votes to John O'Bryant (in the primary) who is a pro-buser... I was in the Army with O'Bryant and believe me, he's not IRISH. He is a Black Man from Roxbury, and believes in forced integration and Forced Busing.[2]

O'Bryant lost. This was not the first time. John O'Bryant had been campaign manager for my unsuccessful attempts in 1961, 1963 and 1965, and had lost in his bid to be state representative in 1964, 1966 and 1968. O'Bryant had been a teacher and a guidance counselor in the school system for fifteen years.

But in 1977, John O'Bryant won, after almost two decades of trying to change the school system. He was the first black person to be elected to the school committee in more than seventy-five years. All those years finally paid off, as O'Bryant got the solid backing of the black community, the white liberal middle class, and a fair number of working class whites who knew John because of his work in the school system. Given his years of experience, John was able to pull together an effective organization that was able to bring out the votes from these constituencies.

THE BLACK POLITICAL TASK FORCE

Although the Massachusetts Black Caucus continued to provide a framework to unify black legislative efforts, particularly around the desegregation plans between 1975 and 1978, it was not cohesive enough to become a major force in organizing people of color in Boston. During this period, I was re-elected in 1974, 1976 and 1978, and was able to push through a major legislation on community economic development as we saw in Chapter 14. But the next link in the institution building stage of black political development was the formation in 1978 of the Black Political Task Force.

John O'Bryant, given his widespread support in the community, was a major force in the establishment of the task force. The purpose of the task force was to increase the political power of people of color.

> ... The Task Force will strive to establish a unified voting constituency among peoples of color... In addition to that, the Black Political Task Force will screen, endorse and work for those candidates committed to the following: 1) The Empowerment of Peoples of Color, 2) The

Redistribution of Goods and Services, 3) An Elevated Standard of Life for Peoples of Color and, 4) Full Employment.[3]
—*BPTF Press Release*, March 25, 1979

The task force brought together, for the first time, community people from over 27 different organizations and agencies. It had a much broader organizational base than any other previous black community organization, and it was not tied to any one person or group. The task force wouldn't just endorse candidates because they were black, and it would also consider endorsing white candidates. Also, the task force pressured people to follow through on their commitment to people of color if they were elected. It was the first organization which could really organize the community, and hold elected officials accountable.

1979 MAYORAL ELECTION

We are here to announce a process which we have initiated... to campaign for mayor of this city. We are stressing a process because we believe we must move away from the practice of politics by personality ... We must turn to a process which builds ongoing decentralization and participation in which we can all take responsibility for managing the affairs of the city in each community. For us the central question is: Whose city is this and who should benefit from its wealth? We are reaching out to people who can answer the question in ways that show their willingness for running the city themselves. Why do I make this announcement? Because I care about this city and I believe in empowerment. Why in the South End at a curbstone? I do this on the street because I worked on the city streets and ultimately I believe it will be these people, here on the streets, who will make the city work for all of us. I make this announcement on this day because Martin Luther King is a symbol of what is best in the United States.[4]
—*BPTF Press Release*, Jan. 15, 1979

Thus began my bid to be mayor of Boston. Over the next eight months, we built support for the campaign by gathering petitions to bring up the Galvin Plan again for a referendum, holding a series of educational forums on to whom this city belonged, and seeking financial support from the widest possible group of supporters. From August 3 through August 5, a black political summit was held with more than sixty people from Boston's black community to review the political position of black Bostonians in the 1970s and 1980s. The three day talks ignited a new level of solidarity, and agreement not to succumb to those forces which seek to divide the black vote. The summit agreed to support my candidacy, and the candidacy of all black aspirants who are willing to be held accountable to the community of color.

In this campaign, the "process" was what we were about. That process included the development of a coalition, and the development of a network of people from different communities willing to take responsibility for creating an organization in their community that would continue independently after my candidacy. The point was to build a structure that would have an impact on other decisions to be made in the community, particularly around the electoral process.

We approached the campaign from the position of having a ward and precinct organization that could have real political power, and from the standpoint of the issues that the various groups from across the city were involved in. Our assessment was that there were many groups attempting to get access, that each group was going after its goals on a one-by-one basis, and they were being played off against each other. Ultimately, these groups have to recognize that, and come together and say, "This is the bottom line," by which I mean the point upon which each group stands, and which all groups have to support and recognize.

The issues were clear—the problems of racial and sexual violence, the problems of access for a variety of groups, control and displacement, employment, energy, the distribution of the wealth of the city, taxes and representation. The central issue of representation and power in the communities was the one around which the neighborhood organizations developed. The issues in their communities were reflected in the positions of the campaign.

Interest groups were also able to develop positions for the campaign, including groups like the Alliance for Rent Control, the Gay Caucus, women's groups, the Third World Jobs Clearing House, the Boston Jobs Coalition, and the elderly. Working with them, we dealt with particular problems, and we developed a set of position papers reflecting proposed solutions.

This was the process. What we said, in effect, was that if people were serious about decentralization, then the campaign process had to be decentralized. If people were serious about community control, then they had to be responsible for taking control. I wanted people to understand where I was coming from in relation to the issues that concerned them. I wanted to talk about my vision of the city, but just as importantly, I wanted to put people on notice that we were going to deal with the issues. Furthermore, we had to get people to realize that it was up to them to make their issue an important one in the campaign. With the rent control issues, and with the Boston Jobs Coalition, things happened on both those issues because I was able to change the nature of the debate during the campaign. I was able to do that because I had the kind of organized support that made it possible.

Looking back over our primary campaign, I think we made the following mistakes. First, if people had really believed in their own power we would have won. The press and many people in the community thought that a black candidate could not win because of the racism in Boston. True, the racial climate in this city did have a very real impact on the campaign. However, I also believe that the issues were most important. The difference was in increased voter registration. People who had not registered came out to register. That's an indication that people were identifying with each other around the issues. A survey after the election determined that more than half of the people who voted for me did so because they identified with the issues. It is clear to me that the candidate who can best frame voter issues in their proper context, and simultaneously possess an organization which goes after the votes successfully can win—and I don't care whether the person is black, white, male, female, short, tall, or one-legged.

Secondly, people did not support their own issues. The 60,000 tenants who were going to be affected by rent decontrol did not vote for me (I supported rent control). Issue oriented groups have not realized the importance of using the electoral process to address their needs. I won 53 precincts—which was more than anybody else won, other than the mayor—but we didn't turn out the volume in those precincts. We were just not geared up in a way that would maximize the turnout in each of the areas. The election came down to a question of organization. White beat Timilty because he had the better organization—that's the only real difference between the two of them. We beat Finnegan because we had the better organization (and we confronted issues). In terms of per capita vote costs, we had the cost of the Finnegan campaign, and one-sixth the cost of the White and Timilty campaigns.

Thirdly, our candidacy failed to help the voters analyze and assess the performance of the incumbent mayor. With respect to the black vote, although we were able to articulate how people were being taken in by Mayor White, they were more afraid of the opposition that Timilty posed. At a meeting at the Trotter school, Doris Bunte confronted the mayor and his supporters in the black community with the fact that in Charlestown and West Roxbury (predominantly white areas) folks were only being taxed at twenty-five percent of the property value, whereas in Roxbury and North Dorchester, they were being taxed at seventy and eighty percent.

In 1975, the Mayor said that if he got the black vote and was re-elected he would change the tax inequality. Four years later there had been no changes. But still the black ministers, who can influence sixty-five percent of the vote in the black community, supported White in the final election, again without getting any firm committment from him. The black vote was taken for granted, while excessive taxation without representation continued.

On the positive side, the "process" worked. People understood each other better. People from different wards or interest groups were able to speak effectively for the concerns of other areas or groups. We had some remarkable examples of this during the campaign. One night when several meetings were scheduled simultaneously, and I couldn't make one in Jamaica Plain, one of the people from Jamaica Plain got up at the meeting and spoke about the campaign and the issues. I was at the Forest Hills Station the next morning, and a woman walked up and said, "We didn't miss you last night," which I took to be a sarcastic comment. But she went on to explain that the guy who had spoken in my place had presented a very clear picture about what the campaign was, and what the issues were. She decided to work for the campaign.

For me, that was a clear indication of the ability of the whole group to begin to erase some of those lines that were between them. People began to speak to the total needs of the group. People began to realize that working together was more effective than working separately. The whole is greater than the sum of its parts. The bottom line is that it's all of us or none of us, and that there's plenty to go around. There is plenty. I know that that flies in the face of energy issues and the like, but the only energy shortage that we're facing today is the energy for goodwill. If we mine that energy, we can produce unlimited amounts of the other kinds of energy.

"The process" left behind a city-wide, neighborhood-based, multi-issue, political organization, The Boston Peoples Organization.

> The Boston Peoples Organization is committed to gaining control of our neighborhoods, jobs and government. Through community, labor, and electoral organizing, we strive to overcome racism, sexism, economic exploitation and all forms of oppression. Furthermore, we are united around a vision of Boston as a community of diverse people who can respect each other, who can work together collectively to solve our common problems, and who will help each other to fulfill our potentials to the fullest extent possible. The Boston Peoples Organization is for power to the people of Boston. It is time to come together, to move out of our isolation, to eliminate the oppressive conditions that surround us, to create a humane society.[5]

The Boston Peoples Organization was formed in late 1979 and early 1980 by folks who had been involved in the campaign, working in the neighborhoods and on issues. They realized that if we were going to turn Boston around in the 1980s we needed to build a city-wide organization which could truly lead to the empowerment of Boston's communities and oppressed peoples.

On December 9, 1979, the anti-racist violence committee of the Boston Peoples Organization held a city-wide planning and informational meeting to begin developing strategies to combat racist violence in Boston. Over 200 people from all over the city, from the communities, churches, and anti-racist organizations came together to plan now to expose the work of the Ku Klux Klan and the Boston Marshalls, and to develop anti-racist training programs in the schools.

The Boston Peoples Organization marks a new stage in the development of a progressive political movement in Boston. Through the Boston Peoples Organization, the black community can unite with other communities and groups fighting for empowerment.

Notes

1. Black voters v. John J. McDonough, U.S. District Court, District of Massachusetts, 1975.
2. *Ibid.*, p. 53.
3. Mel King, *Chain of Change*, South End Press, Boston, Mass. 1980, p. 220.
4. *Ibid.*, p. 220
5. *Ibid.*, p. 224

III

Race, Class, and Politics in the Black Community of Boston

James Jennings

Recently there have appeared a number of studies investigating the relationship of race and class in the black community. With the publication of Wilson's *The Declining Significance of Race* the debate concerning the relative influence of racial and class factors as determinants of various aspects of black life has intensified.[1] This is not a new controversy. Black leaders have continually struggled with the problem of the particular developing relationships between blacks positioned higher and lower on the socioeconomic scale. Frederick Douglass, Booker T. Washington, W.E.B. DuBois, Marcus Garvey, Malcolm X, and Martin Luther King are just a few black leaders who were concerned with this problem. A number of ideas have emerged from contemporary studies of this topic; one is that the middle-class blacks will not encounter labor market discrimination—this is a problem for the poorer blacks who lack vital education skills.[2] Another suggestion, the one that is the focus of this article, is that as blacks obtain higher socioeconomic status, the saliency of race declines in the electoral arena. In other words, as blacks move from the poverty and working-class strata to the ranks of the middle class, they will not think or act politically as blacks, but rather as middle-class individuals. Thus, we should be able to detect significant variations in the electoral behavior and preferences of blacks in different socioeconomic positions.

Boston offers an interesting laboratory to test this idea. This city has a history that points to the presence of what some have referred to as a black "Brahmin" group. In a monumental study of black social life, for instance, Hill argued that the civic influence of these black Brahmins was a result of their having roots in Boston over a lengthy period, dating to the colonial era.[3] But it is not at all clear that historical, political, or economic developments have resulted in a black middle-class sector with attitudes and electoral behavior patterns different from those characteristic of lower socioeconomic blacks; as far as the electoral arena is concerned, race may be the overriding factor in determining black political behavior. One researcher has argued, for example, that to approach black politics as if race was not salient would be a mistake because

> the black majority, located within the working class, view themselves and their political activities through the prism of race, primarily because their children still attend largely black schools, they still live in mostly black neighborhoods, they still attend all black civic and fraternal societies and churches; and because they still perceive whites as a whole discriminating against them because of their race. The black elite, on the other hand, employs race as an ideological and cultural tool to maintain and extend its own influence, its hegemony, over the bulk of working class black society.[4]

As a matter of fact, Marable believes that race remains the "fundamental organizing theme" in the black community. He writes that,

> contrary to the predictions of black sociologist William Wilson and the works of Nathan Glazer and Pat Moynihan, 'race' has not declined in significance. It remains the fundamental organizing theme within black culture and civil society. What has occurred is a different meaning of race, different usages for race, within the contextual framework of black politics.[5]

In other words, race remains salient for both the black working class and the black elite. This means that the political behavior of these sectors will continue to be based on the racial perceptions of its members. It also implies that at times race may weigh more than "class" or socioeconomic background in the political decisions and behavior of blacks in the American city.

Almost two decades after Hill completed her study of Boston's black community, a student of black politics argued that there is "no clear division" between different classes within the black community of Boston because of the ethnic and neighborhood nature of this city. He wrote that

> the city is more than others divided naturally into neighborhoods which have grown out of small towns like Roxbury, Dorchester, Charlestown, Allston, and Brighton, and these provide a basis for some degree of local cohesion.... One characteristic of the black community in

Boston that might be listed as a positive factor is that there is no clear division between middle and more lower class groups within Roxbury; this is probably explained by the scale of the city and the small absolute number of Blacks inside the city.[6]

Although class divisions may not be as pronounced as in other communities, there still exist differences in the socioeconomic characteristics of black people. This is true in Boston, as it is in most of urban America. Fainstein and Fainstein write that "most urban Blacks can be divided into two strata; on the one hand, those with some skill and steady employment who comprise a large proletariat and small bourgeousie; on the other, a poverty stratum, partly employed, often at very low wages, and dependent upon transfer payments for subsistance."[7] In conventional terminology, the "black middle class" is a term that, many times, is used to refer to the former category. In the black community, in other words, members of the working class have been referred to as "middle class" if they own homes, have "good"—i.e., government—jobs, and generally are long-time residents of their neighborhood. For this reason it might be more appropriate to use the term "strata" rather than "class" in discussing the social structure of the black community, as has been suggested by Hamilton.[8] From the class argument, we can expect different strata positions to elicit varying patterns of political behavior and preferences. But it is conceivable that race could have such an effect that we find insignificant differences between the so-called middle-class blacks and poorer black citizens in the electoral arena.

A few contemporary observers have made reference to the role of class in explaining black politics in Boston. Byron Rushing, president of the Museum of Afro-American History in this city, offers that class differences have not predetermined behavior among black people in the political arena. Rushing believes that there is a myth in Boston that assumes that members of a black middle class, made up of the black Brahmins, "pull the important strings." But, says he, individuals delude themselves (perhaps because it is prestigious) into thinking that they wield influence in Boston politics.[9] But others in Boston believe that socioeconomic differences in the black community have created two sets of political interests. In 1979 an editorial in Boston's *Bay State Banner* claimed that the Mel King for Mayor Campaign[10] overlooked the needs and interests of the black middle class in favor of the black poor.[11] This suggested that blacks in the higher and lower rings of the socioeconomic ladder perceived their electoral interests differently from each other. But the data we have compiled suggest that within the black community of Boston socioeconomic differences have generally not been reflected in the electoral arena. As a matter of fact, blacks higher and lower on the socioeconomic ladder seem to be characterized by converging ideological and political preferences. Furthermore, blacks in varying socioeconomic positions generally exhibit common electoral behavior patterns. The remainder of this article describes the data we used to arrive at these conclusions.

METHODOLOGY

A survey of Boston's inner-city electoral precincts produced 18 census tracts with the following characteristics:[12]

- At least 75% of all residents were black in 1970.
- The level of median income ranged from a high of $8,153 in 1970 to a low of $4,389 in the same year.
- The median school years completed ranged from a high of 11.7 years to a low of 9.0 years.
- The rate of homeownership ranged from 25% to 5%.

The aim of our study was to find out if any (or what kind of) relationships existed between these socioeconomic characteristics and the political behavior and preferences of black citizens in selected geopolitical units. Using census tract data, we ranked these electoral units on the basis of median income. Our primary interest was the apparent effect of income on the political behavior of a circumscribed electoral unit. But the fact that we found the level of median schooling highly correlated to the level of median income and homeownership allowed us to make generalizations about the socioeconomic status of the electoral precincts.[13] Our objective was to create a ranking of electoral precincts based on their level of median income and schooling in order to determine whether a relationship between these socioeconomic characteristics and the political behavior patterns for these areas could be found.[14] We wanted to know if we could find significant political differences between "better-off" blacks and what Fainstein and Fainstein refer to as the "poverty stratum" in the black community.

This methodology, which has been used in previous studies, focuses on the "behavior" of an area, such as our electoral precincts, rather than on individuals. Using this approach to examine black voter registration rates in the South, two researchers reported earlier that "this employment of areal rather than individual analysis narrows the question we can examine. Rather than an unqualified examination of the relationship of social and economic characteristics to Negro registration, the effort must be understood to focus on the relationship of social and economic characteristics of given areas (counties) to variations in Negro registration among those areas."[15] Other researchers used this approach in a study of black political behavior in Los Angeles in 1969 and 1973. They found that "although aggregate data do not permit inferences about individual behavior, they can be used to develop generalizations about the voting behavior of electorates with identifiable characteristics." And further, "since cities generally contain relatively clear residential divisions by social status as well as by ethnicity or race, this method permitted the investigation of voter reactions to candidates... in various *segments of the community*."[16] We, too, are measuring variations in the political behavior of electoral "social" areas rather than individuals. The "electorates" that we have separated into "high" and "low" groups are differentiated in their aggregated social and economic characteristics. This forces us to couch our conclusions not in terms of individuals, as is suggested by the Mathews and Prothro study, but rather in terms of electorates. We are not examining political differences between middle-class blacks (as used in the Marxist sense) and lower-class blacks. Our study is merely asking whether black electorates within certain political boundaries exhibit differential electoral patterns based on various socioeconomic indicators. A weakness of this approach is the difficulty of overlapping electoral and census tract boundaries; we tried to overcome this by eliminating electoral units that did not generally fit into the census tract boundaries. Table 1 shows the characteristics of the electoral precincts selected for investigation.

We noticed that there existed significant differences between the upper and lower range of the scale. The top eight electoral precincts had a range of median incomes between $6,335 and $8,153, whereas the bottom five electoral precincts had a much lower range—between $4,389 and $5,533.[17] This latter group also averaged a lower median schooling level (9.4 years) than the top eight electoral precincts (11.8 years). The rate of homeownership was also much higher for the higher-income group than it was for the lower-income group. Again we emphasize that our discussion is based on a sample of two socioeconomic strata in the black community. This is not, necessarily, a study of class distinctions. Our data examines income, schooling, and homeownership differences between geopolitical areas within Boston's black community. Our conclusions pertain only to these areas.

TABLE 1
Socio-Economic Characteristics of Selected Black Electoral Precincts in Boston, 1970

Census Tract	Total Population	Electoral Unit	Percent Black	Median Income	Median Schooling	Percent Home Ownership
820	3,537	W12 P.6	91.0	$8153	11.7 yrs.	25.0
816	1,049	W9 P.5	81.2	7514	12.0	24.0
819	4,191	W12 P.8	92.0	7466	12.0	20.0
815	2,906	W11 P.2,3	78.7	7438	12.0	20.0
901	6,377	W14 P.6	95.0	6896	12.1	23.0
817	4,727	W12 P.3,5	93.0	6625	11.2	17.0
821	5,523	W12 P.9	95.0	6460	11.7	11.0
924	7,489	W14 P.7,9	85.0	6355	11.9	17.0
803	3,285	W12 P.1	77.7	5533	9.7	11.0
709	2,120	W9 P.2	78.0	5469	9.0	5.0
805	1,427	W9 P.3	95.0	4850	9.1	6.0
806	1,889	W9 P.4	90.2	4849	10.2	5.0
804	1,626	W8 P.4	92.5	4389	9.4	1.0

Source: U.S. Bureau of the Census, Census of Population and Housing: 1970 CENSUS TRACTS Final Report PHC (1)-29 Boston, MASS. SMSA and Ward and Precinct Maps for the City of Boston

Is there a relationship between the level of median income found in our political units and the electoral behavior, or ideological preferences, of these units? We have used a number of indicators to illustrate the electoral behavior of our geopolitical units. These include the voter registration rates for 1975 and 1977 and the turnout rates for the following elections in Boston:
- 1975 mayoral preliminary and general elections
- 1977 nonmayoral preliminary and general elections
- 1974 and 1976 state general elections

Race, Class and Politics   45

These electoral contests were chosen because they allow us to observe turnout rates under the different kinds of elections faced by the Boston voter.

Political and ideological preferences refer to the candidate or policy choices of the voters. Our study utilizes several indicators to measure this. These include the choices of black voters to various questions on state ballots in 1976 and the support rate for Proposition 2½—a tax-cutting measure—in 1980, the support rate for two gubernatorial candidates in 1978, and the support rate for State Representative Mel King in the mayoral preliminary election of 1979.

FINDINGS

Examining the information that has been compiled, we can see that there is some relationship between voter registration rates and the level of median income in the areas under study. The correlation coefficient (r) between median income levels and the 1975 voter registration rate was +.60. This is a high value, suggesting that the lower the median income level of an electoral precinct, the lower the voter registration rate tended to be; or the higher the median income, the higher the voter registration rate. In 1977 this changed somewhat. Although the correlation coefficient was still positive, it was much weaker $(r = +.26)$. The lowest registration rates were found among the lower end of the list; the higher rates were found in areas better-off socioeconomically (in median income). Voter registration tended to be higher for those black areas with a high median income, higher median school years completed, and a higher rate of homeownership. This is not, however, a strong relationship. There is not any evidence of a consistent and uniform relationship between the socioeconomic characteristics of predominantly black social areas and voter registration rates in these areas. In fact, a few areas in the lower part of our spectrum had higher voter registration rates than some areas in the higher section did. To summarize, we find that, as would be expected according to standard socioeconomic explanations of political participation, the strata with higher income, education, and homeownership levels were registered in greater proportions; but the relationship in the black electoral precincts we studied is weak, according to the two years we studied.

The next relationship we studied was that between median income and turnout rates in the 1975 mayoral, 1977 city, and 1974 and 1976 state elections. In the 1975 mayoral election the strength of the relationship between income and turnout in the preliminary election was similar to that of the previous relationship—not great at all. The correlation coefficient was +.28. In the mayoral general election this relationship was much stronger ($r = +.576$). This means that there was a greater tendency in the mayoral general election for areas with a higher median income to exhibit higher turnout rates.

TABLE 2
Voter Registration Rates for Selected Black Precincts in Boston, 1975 and 1977

Electoral Unit Ward & Precinct*	Voter Registration Rates 1975	1977
W12 P6	65.3	65.3
W9 P5	57.0	54.4
W12 P8	64.5	57.8
W11 P2,3	54.5	51.3
W14 P6	62.6	54.1
W12 P3,5	67.7	68.5
W12 P9	59.7	58.3
W14 P7,9	49.2	50.6
W12 P1	52.3	63.3
W9 P2	41.0	46.4
W9 P3	48.5	50.1
W9 P4	61.4	57.7
W8 P4	52.7	56.2

*Precincts listed in descending order of median income.
Source: Election Department, Boston, Massachusetts

In the 1977 city preliminary and general election there seemed to be a slightly stronger relationship between median income levels and black voting turnout. The measure for turnout and the preliminary election was +.62, whereas in the general election it was +.55. In this nonmayoral election year, socioeconomic factors may have had a greater influence on black voting practices than in the 1975 mayoral year elections. The last two measures are among the strongest we found in this part of the study. As a matter of fact, except for one area in the bottom five electoral precincts (Ward 12, Precinct 1) all precincts in the higher end of the scale turned out at greater rates than those at the lower end, in the preliminary election of 1977.

This kind of relationship held true for both statewide general elections in 1974 and 1976. The "higher" areas exhibited greater turnout rates for these elections than the "lower" areas for both years. The correlation coefficient for the 1974 general elections was +.49, and for 1976 it was +.40.

TABLE 3
Turnout Rates in Selected Black Precincts in Boston 1975 Mayoral Election, 1977 City Elections, 1974 and 1976 State General Election

Electoral Unit Ward, Precinct*	1975 Mayoral Preliminary	1975 Mayoral General	1977 City Preliminary	1977 City General	State General 1974	State General 1976
W12 P6	38.7	65.1	30.2	46.5	53.2	70.9
W9 P5	42.3	60.7	30.7	48.4	49.1	66.0
W12 P8	44.1	60.2	33.3	51.6	54.1	66.7
W11 P2,3	36.3	56.4	26.2	42.4	47.4	61.9
W14 P6	43.0	60.2	32.2	52.2	50.4	68.1
W12 P3,5	42.7	61.7	33.0	49.7	51.1	67.5
W12 P9	38.9	62.4	31.6	55.2	56.9	67.2
W14 P7,9	32.4	49.3	31.4	40.4	43.0	63.7
W12 P1	41.1	57.1	32.4	50.1	49.8	66.0
W9 P2	38.8	53.6	29.8	43.7	54.6	68.8
W9 P3	43.7	60.4	24.6	40.7	49.1	71.2
W9 P4	34.8	54.3	22.5	41.1	42.6	59.4
W8 P4	34.5	51.5	21.7	35.3	39.3	56.4

*Precincts listed in descending order of median income.
Source: Election Department, Boston, Massachusetts Annual Election Reports, Secretary of State's Office, Commonwealth of Massachusetts

By using these particular measures, we have found that there are slight differences in the electoral behavior or practices of black electorates living in precincts with different levels of median income. From the city elections used for this study it seems that the differences in turnout rates are greater in nonmayoral rather than mayoral years. We cannot conclude, however, that median income levels have a consistently strong, positive influence on registration or turnout rates. And again we note that we are not really comparing two "classes" of black voters. We are examining differences in black geopolitical units, based on socioeconomic "strata" rather than classes.

Now we shall look at the "electoral preferences" of black people living in political units with varying socioeconomic characteristics. We have selected a number of measures for this. These include the following city and state elections:

- Two proposals to amend the state constitution in the November 1976 state election.
- The vote in favor of Proposition 2½% in November 1980.
- The support rate for Michael Dukakis in the Democratic party primary election for governor in September 1978.
- The support rate for Edward Hatch in the general election for governor in November 1978.
- The support rate for Mel King in the mayoral preliminary election in September 1979.

These measures were selected because together they are representative of the kinds of public policy issues that periodically come before the voters in Boston. These measures should give us some indication of the relationship between socioeconomic characteristics and the electoral preferences of black voters.

In the state election of November 1976 there were two constitutional amendments proposed that might serve as indicators of the policy preferences of the black community on women's rights and gun control issues. Part of Question 1 read as follows:

> The proposed amendment would provide that equality under the law may not be denied or abridged on the basis of sex, race, color, creed, or national origin. . . .

Wards 9, 12, and 14, representing the bulk of the black community, voted 76.1% in favor of this amendment. The other voters in Boston, however, gave this amendment only a 54.1% rate of support. Black voters, considered as one group, took a more liberal stand on equal rights for women than the white voters of Boston did. If we examine black voters according to our model, we find that this held true across the black community—regardless of the socioeconomic characteristics of the electorate.

There were only slight differences in the preferences of black voters in the various precincts for equal rights. The correlation coefficient between median income and a "yes" rate on this question was +.25.

In 1976 the voters of Boston had an opportunity to endorse

legislation that would "prohibit the possession, ownership, or sale of any weapon for which a shot or bullet can be discharged and which has a barrel length of less than sixteen inches." Here we find a similarity in the preferences of black and white voters. Whereas 40% of the voters in Wards 9, 12, and 14 supported a prohibitioN against private hand gun possession, 40% of the voters outside these wards also favored this legislation. Within our socioeconomic categories in the black community the response rate to this question was almost identical. The correlation coefficient was +.10, suggesting a weak relationship between the median income of an area and the policy preference on banning private hand guns.

TABLE 4
Support Rate for Selected Issues in Selected Black Precincts in Boston: "Yes" Rate

Electoral Unit Ward, Precinct*	'Equal Rights,' State Constitutional Amendment November 1976	'Hand Guns' State Constitutional Amendment November 1976	Proposition 2½ November 1980
W12 P6	76.6	44.1	36.3
W9 P5	78.4	39.8	26.9
W12 P8	75.5	41.0	77.6
W11 P2,3	74.3	37.8	21.3
W14 P6	81.2	41.7	32.2
W12 P3,5	75.3	46.2	26.7
W12 P9	77.4	41.6	39.3
W14 P7,9	75.7	35.7	57.9
W12 P1	77.2	32.8	43.7
W9 P2	79.8	49.3	36.9
W9 P3	77.6	43.9	25.0
W9 P4	66.9	37.5	24.0
W8 P4	75.4	39.0	27.0

*Precincts listed in descending order of median income
Source: Annual Election Reports, Secretary of State's Office, Commonwealth of Massachusetts

Another important public policy choice faced by the black voters in Boston was whether to approve Proposition 2½%, which required that property taxes in Massachusetts be limited to no more than 2½% of assessed valuation, thereby necessitating cuts in social and human services; this proposal passed in Boston by a comfortable margin: 92,068 to 69,422 or 57% in favor and 43% opposed. This was reversed in the black community, where the measure was defeated by 69%. The vote was only slightly influenced by the socioeconomic characteristics of the black social areas under study ($r = +.27$). It seems that even the rate of homeownership in these social areas contributed little to the policy preferences of black electorates on Proposition 2½; the correlation value between homeownership and a "yes" vote was weak ($r = +.22$).

In the Democratic party's gubernatorial primary on September 19, 1978, Michael S. Dukakis lost Boston to Edward J. King by 13,497 votes out of a total of 89,646 votes cast. Dukakis was recognized as the liberal candidate by the media; King was considered conservative in his political philosophy. In the black community, however, Dukakis beat King by an almost two-to-one margin. While the governor obtained 58% of the black vote, challenger King received 29%, and the third gubernatorial candidate, Barbara Ackerman, received 12%. Among white voters, or rather voters outside Wards 9, 12, and 14, Dukakis' proportion of the vote dropped to 38.7%, while King enjoyed a 55.2% support rate. The percentage figures for the predominantly white wards were reversed in the black wards. If the Dukakis and King candidacies were approached in terms of varying political philosophies and public policy preferences, then we would have yet another instance in which black and white voters perceive their interests differently in the electoral arena. How did black voters respond to these two candidates when we consider the median income levels of our selected social areas? We find that the higher socioeconomic strata tended to support Dukakis at a slightly higher rate than the lower socioeconomic strata did. The correlation coefficient for this relationship was $+.45$. This means that Dukakis tended to do better among the higher median income areas in the black community than among the lower median income residential pockets. This is interesting because it suggests that generally better-off areas may be more liberal than poorer areas in the black community. We will say more about this after examining the next relationship.

What did black voters do after the conservative challenger defeated the incumbent governor in this election? In Wards 9, 12, and 14, blacks decided to vote for the Republican party candidate, who was perceived as more liberal than Edward King, the winner of the Democratic party nomination. The vote in these areas was 74.2% for Hatch and 25.7% for King. Thus, despite the fact that King won the Democratic party nomination and that most blacks selected this party label over the Republican party label, they were sophisticated enough to switch for the candidate perceived as liberal. The support for Hatch was dispersed among all the black precincts. But the "high" group did support him at a higher rate than the "low" group. The correlation coefficient here was +.52. Again we find that the black voters in the higher median income areas seemed more liberal (and sophisticated) than black voters in the poorer sectors of the black community.

The last measure we looked at is the proportion of black voters

TABLE 5
Support Rate for Selected Candidates in Selected Black Precincts in Boston

Electoral Unit Ward, Precinct*	Dukakis Democratic Gubernatorial Primary September 1978	Hatch Gubernatorial Election November 1978	King Mayoral Preliminary Election 1979
W12 P6	70.0	80.2	51.9
W9 P5	76.6	81.0	56.0
W12 P8	56.0	78.0	50.9
W11 P2,3	74.7	77.7	59.6
W14 P6	65.5	74.0	58.2
W12 P3,5	66.9	71.5	56.0
W12 P9	75.6	82.7	51.1
W14 P7, 9	66.1	71.9	48.5
W12 P1	63.2	73.1	58.7
W9 P2	62.4	73.6	64.7
W9 P3	65.2	78.5	64.0
W9 P4	69.0	69.2	56.9
W8 P4	53.8	68.7	47.5

*Precincts listed in descending order of median income.
Source: Annual Election Report, Secretary of State's Office, Commonwealth of Massachusetts Election Department, City of Boston

supporting State Representative Melvin King in the September 1979 mayoral preliminary campaign. Mel King was recognized as a strong advocate for the poor in Boston. He finished the race in third place, behind Kevin White and Joseph Timilty, with 15% of the vote (17,401 votes). In the black community King received a slightly higher rate of support from the "low" group than he did from the "high" group. But the correlation coefficient ($r = -.19$) shows this to be a weak relationship.

CONCLUSION

We found that there are indeed some slight differences in the electoral behavioral of black voters when we separate them into high and low socioeconomic areal categories based on the level of median income. These slight differences include turnout rates for primary and general elections and voter registration rates. The higher the socioeconomic status of the black electorate in Boston, the higher the turnout and registration rates for that area tended to be; however, this relationship was not found to be consistent among all the areas selected for study. Despite these differences in electoral behavior or "practices," our areal model does not suggest any significant political schisms based on the socioeconomic indicators used. Black voters tended to vote the same way on a number of city and state ballot questions, support the same candidates at both the city and state level, and vote the liberal preference on both issues and candidates regardless of socioeconomic background. In addition, there is some evidence that the higher a black voter is on the socioeconomic scale, the greater his or her tendency will be to vote the liberal position on various issues and candidates. Our model also suggests that black voters will tend to support black candidates regardless of some socioeconomic factors. If this model can be used as an indication of class differences in the black community, then our data show that socioeconomic criteria are not as salient as race in determining the political behavior and preferences of black voters.

These findings are generally similar to those for other cities. Hamilton discovered in a study of Harlem politics in New York City that one finds "social strata" rather than "classes" in this black community.[18] He analyzed and compared the electoral practices and choices of six low socioeconomic groups with six high socioeconomic groups. The former were characterized by a median income of

$4,100, an average of 8.4 school years completed, and a 70% rate of receiving public assistance or working low-income jobs; the latter were characterized by a median income of $8,700, an average of 12.1 school years completed, and a 7.5% rate of employment in public sector jobs. He found that whereas the voter registration rates for the low group were greater than the rates for the high group (75-80% compared to 45-55%) there were insignificant differences in the electoral preferences of these two groups. He writes, "What I found was that middle-status blacks were not only closer to the black lower-status voters, but the middle class blacks were to the left (or more liberal) than all the other groups.... In other words, my research, to date, does not show that black middle class voters tend to be more conservative than black lower class voters—or tend to behave more like their white middle class counterparts than like the black lower class. In fact, just the opposite."[19] This finding was also supported by the Hahn, et al. investigation of the mayoralty election in Los Angeles in 1969 and 1973. They reported that

> in both the 1969 and the 1973 elections, the demographic correlates of the vote for mayor were remarkably similar.... Perhaps the most notable feature of both analyses was the strong and direct association between the vote for Bradley and the non-white proportion of the population, which appeared to overshadow the other variables. As the percentage of non-white residents of an area increased, the vote for Bradley also increased. Furthermore, this association was not affected by socioeconomic characteristics such as income or education.[20]

From this they concluded that "the data, therefore, did not corroborate the frequently expressed fear that the electoral choices of the middle- or upper-middle class black areas might diverge from the voting patterns of working-class black areas, or that they might provide reduced support for black candidates."[21] These conclusions support our findings. In Boston we found large socioeconomic differences in the black social areas we selected for study, but these differences were not reflected in black political behavior as may be the case for whites.[22] From our information, we argue that race carries greater weight in determining the electoral preferences and behavior of the black community in this city than socioeconomic background does. This is not to argue that in other arenas we would not find differences between the so-called middle-class blacks and poor blacks. But in the electoral arena blacks are voting in ways that suggest similar political perceptions regardless of socioeconomic background.

These findings are interesting in light of recent studies suggesting the declining relative weight of race and increasing weight of class in determining the level of discrimination encountered by black people. Our findings indicate that at least in the electoral arena we cannot yet dispel racial perceptions as an overriding influence on black political behavior. Socioeconomic background may not be as strong as other factors in determining black political behavior in the American city, as has been suggested by some studies.

Notes

Special thanks to Dr. Ricardo Millet for useful suggestions in the completion of this study and to Mr. Sheldon Fisher for assisting the author with data collection.

1. William J. Wilson, *The Declining Significance of Race*, Chicago: University of Chicago Press, 1977.
2. See Wilson, op. cit.; Richard Freeman, *The Black Elite*, New York: Carnegie Foundation, 1976; and Thomas Sowell, *Race and Economics*, New York: David McKay Co., Inc. 1972.
3. Adelaide Hill, *The Negro Upper Class in Boston*, Ph.D. diss., Radcliffe College, 1952.
4. Manning Marable, *From the Grassroots* Boston: South End Press, 1980, p. 224.
5. Ibid., p. 224.
6. Michael K. Marshall, "Community Control of Schools in Boston: Prelude to a New Pluralism," Senior thesis, Harvard University, 1969, p. 11.
7. Norman I. Fainstein and Susan S. Fainstein, *Urban Political Movements: The Search for Power by Minority Groups in American Cities*, New Jersey: Prentice-Hall, Inc., 1974, p. 3.
8. Charles V. Hamilton, "Race and Class in American Politics," Lecture delivered at Columbia University School of Journalism, October 9, 1978.
9. Interview with Byron Rushing, president of the Museum of Afro-American History in Boston, Massachusetts, on July 22, 1980.
10. Mel King was a black state representative who ran for the mayoralty in the fall of 1979; the first black candidate to run for this office was City Councilman Thomas Atkins in 1971.
11. *Bay State Banner*, September 12, 1980.
12. The data presented here is compiled from the U.S. Bureau of the Census, Census of Population and Housing: 1970 *Census Tracts* Final Report PHC (1)-29, Boston Mass. SMSA and Annual Reports of the Department of Elections, Boston, Massachusetts.

13. We measure only the correlative value between a social area's level of median income and various electoral characteristics; owing to the multicollinearity between median income, median schooling and homeownership that was found, we made generalizations based solely on the level of median income.

14. A measure of r was used to determine the correlation value. Pearson's Product Moment correlation coefficient (r) is a statistical measurement of the relationship between two interval or lower-level variables. A value close to ± 1.0 (such as .85) suggests that there is some relationship (it could be positive or negative) between the variables under study (usually an independent variable and a dependent one). A value close to 0 (such as .11) suggests that there is a relationship but it is extremely weak. Correlation does not mean causation; Pearson's r represents the extent to which the same individuals or events occupy the same relative position on two variables. A positive relationship means that high scores on one variable tend to be correlated with high scores on a second variable. A negative relationship means that low scores on one variable tend to be correlated with high scores on the other variable.

Note that all correlation values reported here were found to be statistically significant at the .05 level of significance. A "T statistic" was used to determine statistical significance. See Richard P. Runyon and Audrey Haber, *Fundamentals of Behavioral Statistics*, Reading, MA.: Addison-Wesley Publishing Co., 1972, and William Mendenhall, Lyman Ott, and Richard F. Larson, *Statistics: A Tool for the Social Sciences*, North Scituate, MA.: Duxbury Press, 1974.

15. Donald Mathews and James Prothro, "Social and Economic Factors and Negro Voter Registration in the South," *American Political Science Review*, March 1963, p. 26.

16. Harlan Hahn, David Klingman, and Harry Pachon, "Cleavages, Coalitions, and the Black Candidate: The Los Angeles Mayoralty Elections of 1969 and 1973," in Harlan Hahn and Charles Levine, *Urban Politics: Past, Present and Future*, New York: Longman, 1980, p. 155. See the following for an additional explanation of this methodology: Harold F. Goldsmith and Elizabeth L. Unger, *Social Areas: Identification Procedures Using 1970 Census Data*. This study was published by the Mental Health Study Center, National Institute of Mental Health (NIMH) in May 1972.

17. The median income for all black families in the United States was $6,279 in 1970. U. S. Bureau of the Census *Social and Economic Characteristics of the Black Population*, 1972 Current Population Reports, Series P-60 no. 85, December 1972.

18. Charles V. Hamilton, "Race and Class in American Politics" (Lecture delivered at Columbia University School of Journalism, October 9, 1978).

19. Ibid. p. 8.

20. Hahn, op. cit., p. 158.

21. Ibid., p. 158.

22. A number of works have found evidence of strong relationships between the class backgrounds and the political behavior of Americans. See the following: Eulau Heinz, "Perceptions of Class and Party in Voting Behavior: 1952," *American Political Science Review*, June 1955; Angus Campbell et. al.,

The American Voter, New York: Wiley, 1960; Robert E. Lane, *Political Life*, New York: The Free Press, 1959; Sidney Verba and Norman H. Nie, *Participation in America: Political Democracy and Social Equality*, New York: Harper and Row, 1972; Lester Milbraith, *Political Participation*, Chicago: Rand McNally, 1965; Seymore Lipset, *Political Man*, Garden City, New York: Doubleday, 1960.

IV

Urban Machinism and the Black Voter: The Kevin White Years
James Jennings

One of the major functions of America's big-city mayors is to provide "political managerialism" beneficial to powerful economic interests. An unstated responsibility of political leadership of cities is to maintain a stable environment in which banking, real estate, academic, commercial, and media conglomerates can realize their political and economic goals. This becomes especially evident during periods of fiscal crisis, when big-city mayors sacrifice the interests of the poor and the powerless to the well-being of organizations that own and manage wealth.

Although political managerialism has increasingly replaced "political leadership" as the major function of big-city mayors since World War II, city halls in earlier periods of American history also provided this important service. But it was the political machine and its influential bosses, rather than strictly the mayor's office, that provided it.

The difference between earlier periods and the post-World War II era lies in the fact that it was easier to provide political managerialism in the 19th century and the first 30 years or so of the 20th century. The political machine before World War II provided a "network that connected the 'boss' to both the upper and lower class of urban society. To the upper class, the boss supplied utility and street car franchises, construction contracts, and other juicy patronage plums. To the [lower class] immigrants whose votes kept the machine in power, the boss 'ward heelers' provided petty jobs, turkeys at Christmas, and other minor favors."[1] Today, big-city mayors and their political organizations must perform similar duties. They must create and maintain a healthy environment for the economic interests of powerful groups. But to do so is far more complex today. The mayor's office must be able to manage the demands of labor upon industry, including the demands of public-sector workers; it must be able to maintain the allegiance of volatile white working-class groups, using either city hall patronage or the subtle threat of black and Latino "invasions"; and, increasingly since the 1960s, in most larger American cities, mayors must contain the growing black and Latino groups whose social and economic interests cannot be responded to within the traditional political framework of urban America.

The big-city mayor, in effect, is the hired manager of the "metropolitan establishment":

> This is a multi-level network of power centers (including institutional hierarchies) that are held together less by formal control than by mutual interests, shared ideologies, and accepted procedures for mediating their endless conflicts. It is both public government and private government, permanent but constantly changing, and seen in various degrees of visibility and invisibility. It is a network of government officials, corporate managers, law firms, accounting firms, wealthy individuals, professional associations, chambers of commerce, union leaders, dependable academics, think tanks, media executives, and, last and occasionally least, the leaders of some of the many political machines in the metropolitan area.[2]

This metropolitan establishment exercises considerable influence over the daily lives of powerless poor and working-class people. The control exercised by the metropolitan establishment over public policy "is invisible and unelected... the power of this interlocking network of elites is based on the control of institutions, money, property, and the law-making process." It endures "no matter who the voters elect as mayor, governor, or president. Its collective power, when organized, is greater than the elected, representative government."[3]

These are powerful forces, indeed; and to be sure, a mayor cannot make much of a difference in the poor quality of life in the nation's cities. As Greer writes, "The political and economic priorities of our society make it likely that these difficulties will continue. Moreover, there is currently no political coalition with any prospect of changing these priorities to the extent necessary to compel a sharp alteration of the existing urban plight."[4] Further, "The difference in the daily life of the average city dwellers made by a change in the occupant of the mayor's office is too small to be noticeable."[5] He also maintains, "The leaders of contemporary political machines have been quite unwilling to share power with the black community. Blacks are rarely given important parts within the machines themselves, and even more rarely appointed beyond the token level to key positions in city government."[6]

But the *structural* position of the mayor's office can give the occupant opportunities to initiate political decisions that begin to favor the interests of the powerless. Before this can happen, however, blacks must be organized around an agenda of progressive issues. And black leaders must be aware of all the political resources that big-city mayors will use to obstruct the growth of a black progressive politics.

The office of the big-city mayor represents the "dominant force in the formal governance structure, . . . the central figure in the visible policy network."[7] But just as significant,

> The mayors also have ample linkages to the less visible parts of the establishment. These linkages, especially those with corporative management and the super rich, are often forged through fund raising drives for election campaigns. Other links are developed through "lend-an-executive" technical-assistance programs, where management skills and other forms of technology are transferred from the private to the public needs.[8]

On the top layer of this metropolitan establishment sit the "super rich" and their corporate managers. At the middle level are those "who provide the material, intellectual, and leadership resources that keep the establishment functioning." And "on the junior ring sit most party machines, bureaucrats, and union leaders." Finally, "There are also those outside the establishment network—the unemployed, the poor, the minorities, and others who are unable to influence, or receive tangible benefits from, the transactions of the metropolitan establishment."[9] Thus while the mayor is expected to represent the electorate, he or she must also be responsible to organized interests. The former encourages a mantle of leadership, the latter an opportunity to be a good manager.

Because of the growing influence of the big institutional networks, the political-managerial function of big-city mayors has become more pronounced in recent years. Perhaps one of the most prominent examples of this is the role of New York City's former mayor, Abraham Beame, during that city's fiscal crisis in the early 1970s. Mayor Beame was reduced to acting as a messenger boy between the corporate representatives on the Emergency Financial Control Board (EFCB), the Municipal Assistance Corporation (MAC), and Governor Hugh Carey. The one individual who was elected by the voters of New York City had very little influence in deciding the political and economic future of the city—his leadership role was transformed completely into a managerial one.[10]

This kind of leadership transformation has been resisted in a few cities. A handful of populist-oriented mayors have tried to adopt advocacy roles in favor of poor and working-class citizens; they have sought to avoid the managerial role imposed upon mayors all over the country. In most cases these mayors have not been successful up to this point in American urban history. Either they have not been allowed to be effective, or have been defeated when facing re-election. And in more than one case, progressive mayors have been exposed to physical attack and various forms of legal harassment.[11]

Despite these defeats, an increasing number of groups are willing to take on the metropolitan establishment. They are increasingly turning towards the electoral arena as the place to challenge the powerful and wealthy. The first major step in confronting these interests is the capture of the mayor's office by progressive forces. As traditional mayors increasingly face progressive challenges, they will find themselves doing battle with groups seeking not merely to replace them, but also to introduce a new kind of politics in urban government. In Boston, such a battle has already emerged.

Mayor Kevin White and his personal political machine came to be recognized as one of the most powerful in America.[12] In 1979, black, white, and Latino progressive groups attempted to dislodge White from power. While two of the major challengers to White sought merely to replace him with other alternative "personalities," groups representing State Representative Mel King spearheaded a progressive challenge to politics-as-usual. These efforts are continuing in local and citywide elections.

The significance of this incipient, popularly based electoral uprising is that it will be repeated in other major cities. Underlying the new challenge to entrenched power in the electoral arena is the feeling that "change for the better comes only when movements of common people rally around an idea and create new leaders from the bottom up," and that "movements of ordinary people, acting out of self-interest, can write law. The moral authority of exemplary action can change lives."[13] But these ideas will be resisted by big-city mayors and their political machines.

Such resistance can be witnessed in Boston. During his tenure, Mayor White performed his politician-managerial responsibilities superbly; he adopted and implemented policies that favored the powerful and wealthy and hurt the poor. His major accomplishment was the development of an atmosphere that was considered positive by big business interests; most of the mayor's more important actions were taken at the expense of those at the lower end of the socioeconomic ladder. Under his leadership, various electoral practices and processes were used to discourage and circumscribe any significant level of progressive black political activism.

A few community activists have argued that the black community in Boston has not been aggressive politically; that blacks have not participated in the electoral arena as much as they should; and that therefore it is understandable that white politicians have not been as responsive as they should be to black voters. Furthermore,

> Until black voters begin to demand more jobs and appointments for their support, politicians will continue to seek the black vote only as a necessary balance of power to guarantee the margin of victory.... Until black voters are secure enough and militant enough to demand that white politicians take a strong liberal stand on the racial issue, even at the risk of defeat, the white politicians will continue to compromise and postpone the inevitable day of full black participation in the administration of American democracy.[14]

But the black community of Boston has a long history of demanding equal treatment by city hall. The fact that blacks have not been as organized and mobilized as they should be is not an attitudinal problem; rather, it is a consequence of the depressing effects of various political decisions made by Kevin White between 1967 and 1983. Under his leadership, city hall utilized four general approaches to prevent the development of a progressively oriented black politics in Boston. These included: 1) the selective use of city hall patronage and public dollars for purposes of reward and punishment; 2) manipulation of public relations techniques to preserve the "liberal" image of the mayor; 3) manipulation of various electoral processes, such as voter registration procedures and city elections; and 4) the nurturing of "cooperative" black political leadership. Each of these approaches has been used to discourage black political activism that city hall found threatening.

Numerous instances in Boston politics show how city hall patronage and public dollars were used to strengthen the White regime, by rewarding a loyalist or punishing an enemy. The mayor's use of summer youth funds to reward his political friends and workers is one example; another was his threat to cut off city funds to the programs of uncooperative Latino human service leaders during the mayoral campaign of 1979. That same year White also provided financial grants to a few black ministers who agreed to support his re-election effort. Cooperative black leaders were appointed to prestigious boards and commissions while the more independent ones were banished from city hall-controlled processes.

Political fear prevented some blacks from becoming identified with issues in ways not sanctioned by city hall under Kevin White. The *Boston Globe* and the *Boston Herald* stated in various articles that the mayor had control over money and jobs that he used to punish those not loyal to him. Another paper, the *Boston Phoenix*, commented that this affected all sectors in Boston politics and influenced the endorsements White received in his 1979 mayoral bid: "The power blocs who have no votes but who carry a great deal of influence—the banks, the utilities, the insurance companies, the major real estate houses are with White out of fear more than anything else."[15] So it was with some elements in the black community.

The fear of political reprisals may be a real obstacle to increased black political participation in Boston. Fear was described as one of White's most important political resources by every black elected official in Boston—one stated that fear of political and economic reprisals is what helped to maintain the paternalistic relationship between some black leaders and city hall. He explained that since the economic foundations of blacks in Boston is so dependent on white power structures, black leaders were not willing to participate in political activities that might be viewed as threatening by the White machine.

Black former state Senator Bill Owens offered an example of the mayor's style in dealing with those not loyal to him. Owens was personally assured by White that he would have a large amount of influence with the economic development of the Blue Hill Commission in Roxbury in the mid-1970s, but when the two were involved in a conflict over the Commission's priorities, White ignored his promise and turned to the now-deceased Robert Forst, believed by Owens to be more cooperative with the mayor. Another black elected official, state Representative Doris Bunte, had a similar experience upon her appointment as a board member to the Boston Housing Authority. After Bunte refused to follow White's dictates, he attempted to punish her by removing her and making it clear that she was to be regarded as persona non grata in city hall.

The threat of reprisal for not supporting the mayor or his policies may have been subtle, but the message was always quite clear. There was an understanding in Boston that if you worked for city hall or desired any governmental assistance, you were expected to support the mayor; if you didn't follow this rule, then your job or grant would be given to more cooperative individuals. This is why in 1979 some members of the Vulcan Society (an association of black firemen in Boston) told a Mel King campaign worker seeking their support that while as an organization they would not openly defy the mayor, they would individually and "quietly" work and vote for Mel King. In Boston, political fear was not completely based on violence, as it might be in other cities, but rather on the professional and economic dependence of black citizens on city hall. The political vulnerability of blacks working for city hall produced the same effect: independent black political behavior was discouraged and punished.

The other approaches that were available to the White machine may not have been as obvious during certain periods as the one just discussed, but they were important in helping to establish the environment under which black politics has developed. They may even have been more important, because their utility was not merely in keeping a manager like White in power, but also in maintaining a political environment that did not encourage black-led challenges to the overall workings and interests of the metropolitan establishment.

Bachrach and Baratz argue that a public image can be manipulated by those who enjoy power so that the powerless do not question the arrangements supporting the powerful.[16] This means that political imagery or symbolism can be used to prevent blacks from raising these questions, and at the same time keep blacks from realizing their potential for political power. In urban politics a "set of predominant values, beliefs, rituals, and procedures ... operate systematically and consistently to the benefit of certain persons and groups at the expense of others.[17] Those groups with power seek to maintain their positions by discouraging public discussion of issues that might threaten the structures and processes supporting their base of power. An important "resource" used to maintain conditions for keeping intact a particular arrangement is "non-decision-making": any issues that do emerge must not question the structures underlying certain processes of interaction between the powerless and the powerful:

> The primary method for maintaining a given mobilization of bias is non-decision making. A non-decision, as we define it, is a decision that results in suppression or thwarting of a latent or manifest challenge to the values or interest of decision makers. To be more nearly explicit, non-decision making is a means by which demands for change in the existing allocation of benefits and privileges in the community can be suffocated before they gain access to the relevant decision-making arena or failing all these things, maimed or destroyed in the decision implementing stage of the policy process.[18]

This "non-decision-making" approach to public policy in Boston was partially dependent upon the mayor's liberal reputation. White's liberal image was used to suffocate issues that might question that paternalistic political relationship between the black community and city hall. Even in his dealing with the problem of racial violence, White used his liberal reputation to dilute black efforts to create greater degrees of racial harmony in Boston. According to Reverend William Alberts of Boston, the major accomplished this by "redefining problems" in ways that rendered them innocuous to his political position. This is another form of non-decision-making. Alberts writes, "A key dynamic of systemic racism is the ability of its leaders to *redefine the problem* in terms acceptable and favorable to them and their constituents."[19] In this way, city hall under White manipulated the black community and some of its leaders so that they did not consider political options that would threaten the mayor's power. An example of this is the way racial violence was continually approached by the mayor's office; such incidents were handled as isolated occurrences. According to Micho Spring, one of White's confidants and a deputy mayor, this was the most effective way to deal with racial violence.[20] This approach kept the public from seeing both the relationship between racial harassment and broader public policies of the mayor's office, and the connection between racial violence and the necessity of political mobilization with a progressive agenda.

"Political symbolism" was indeed an important resource for White's machine; it was vital in attempting to discourage black political activism within a progressive framework. Through subtle manipulation of media exposure and public relations events, White portrayed himself as a relatively liberal mayor who could be responsive to the needs of black people. Unfortunately, some black voters allowed themselves to be fooled by the mayor's liberal image. During the mayoral general election in 1979, for example, some black supporters of White voiced the opinion that he "tries hard." Other blacks, while agreeing that the black community had been short-changed in terms of city services and that racial violence was increasing in Boston, supported White because "he has done the most that he can do."

When blacks criticized White's affirmative action performance in the 1979 mayoral race, he cleverly suggested that his opponent, state Senator Joseph Timilty, had not hired any blacks to his staff. Of course he did not mention that Timilty was not under the same obligation for affirmative action as was the mayor of Boston. White's—and indeed Boston's—historical liberal image slowed the politicization of blacks in Boston. Mayoral races that pitted White against Louise Day Hicks, or Joseph Timilty—who have either been openly antagonistic to black interests or, in the latter case, ignored black Bostonians—served to emphasize to black voters White's liberal image. This explains some of the previous attachments of the black community to city hall—attachments that hindered the politicization of the black community.

The "political climate" in Boston since 1967 allowed Kevin White to use his liberal credentials to depress black political participation. Danigelis explains how the political milieu of a city affects the actualization of black political power:

> The political climate theory of black political behavior maintains that different areas and time periods in this country's history can be characterized by political climates intolerant or supportive of or indifferent to black political participation and that, as a consequence, blacks have faced differing levels of political climate. This type of political climate, therefore, is the key to understanding the political profile of black Americans.[21]

Different kinds of political climates have elicited various black political patterns:

Where laws and feelings are highly hostile toward black participation in politics, an intolerant political climate should be found. A supportive political climate involves at worst incomplete white resistance to black participation and at best active white support. A neutral or ambiguous political climate, where discriminatory barriers are absent or basically irrelevant to black political participation, probably is found throughout much of the North during the period between 1959 and 1972.[22]

Boston can be described as a city in the third category. This political climate effectively depresses black political aspirations and maintains black political noninvolvement. An ambiguous political climate allows ineffective mayoral leadership in the area of race relations to seem more important than it actually is. When the climate is not openly hostile toward black political participation, insignificant instances of leadership are perceived as important, because these actions are contrasted to a hostile or neutral political climate.

Other kinds of political resources were used by the mayor's office to discourage black political participation from threatening the metropolitan establishment. From 1950 to 1982, Boston was organized under an at-large electoral system, which effectively prevented black candidates from winning seats on the city council and school committee. Two exceptions were John O'Bryant, the first black to sit on Boston's school committee in the 20th century (elected in 1977), and Tom Atkins, who sat on the city council between 1967 and 1971. The discriminatory effect of at-large elections was illustrated vividly in the 1979 city elections, when three black candidates won runoff positions but lost in the general election because they did not have enough resources to appeal to the general electorate.

In 1980 the mayor of Boston stated in his inaugural address that he would attempt to change the at-large system of voting so that neglected neighborhoods and minorities could begin to enjoy access to their government.[23] But he did virtually nothing to encourage the adoption of this kind of reform. In November 1982, the voters of Boston narrowly approved a referendum to change the at-large system to one based on nine district seats and four at-large seats in city council and school committee elections. The mayor and his machine took a hands-off position toward adoption of this reform. The advertising campaigns and vote-pulling had been done by the Committee for District Representation (CDR), an organization composed of black, Latino, and white community activists from various parts of Boston.

CDR collected the 22,000 signatures to place the question on the ballot and coordinated the effort to pull out favorable voters. While an earlier 1977 reform effort was directed in part by the mayor and his machine, the 1982 reform effort was spearheaded by progressive organizations having no connection with the mayor's office.

Although Boston instituted a district-based system of voting to take effect in the 1983 city council and school committee elections, the district lines that were finally adopted and approved by the mayor discriminated against the black and Latino community. The Black Political Task Force, an organization of black and Latino community activists, and the CDR objected to the final district boundaries for two reasons.[24] First, the district map relied on the state census of population published in 1975, rather than the federal population census taken in 1980. The former not only overestimated the total population of Boston by more than 100,000 persons, but also underestimated the size and growth of the black and Latino population in Boston. In addition, some predominantly black and Latino areas were placed in districts with a history of racial hostility and violence towards these groups; thus, even under a district-based system of voting, thousands of blacks and Latinos in locations like the South End and North Dorchester were in effect disenfranchised because they were placed in virtually all-white, hostile districts in neighborhoods like South Boston, South Dorchester, Savin Hill, and Neponset. The mayor approved the final map, although the only black city councilor raised these concerns as did a number of black, Latino, and progressive white community groups.

Another electoral process under the mayor's control and leadership that has been used to discourage black political mobilization is voter registration procedures. In Boston, this process is so cumbersome that effective voter registration drives in the black community require herculean efforts and extensive resources. If these resources are not available, voter registration will not be given the attention it requires— unless it is to the advantage of city hall to do so. Voter registration should be an "easy" process for potential black voters to become actual voters. This is crucial for the development of black political power. But voter registration procedures make it very difficult to increase the number of black voters in Boston.[25] During nonelection periods, for instance, potential voters must register in person at city hall or the various neighborhood "little city halls" under the Office of

68   FROM ACCESS TO POWER

Public Services, and only on weekdays between the hours of nine and five o'clock. These hours are extended only two weeks before an upcoming election.[26]

As suggested by the following table, these arrangements work to

TABLE 6
Voter Registration Rates in Boston
By Neighborhoods, 1977-1980*

Ward/Neighborhood	1977 (%)	1978 (%)	1980 (%)
Ward 20, West Roxbury, Roslindale	76.7%	79.9%	74.7%
Ward 2, Charlestown	72.9	77.3	70.7
Ward 7, South Boston, Dorchester	72.3	77.3	67.0
Ward 6, South Boston	70.9	76.0	67.3
Ward 16, Dorchester, Neponset, Cedar Grove	70.8	75.3	68.8
Ward 18, Hyde Park, Mattapan	69.1	73.1	64.2
Ward 1, East Boston	62.2	66.3	65.2
Ward 19, Roslindale	62.1	67.2	62.6
Ward 17, Dorchester	60.8	66.8	52.7
Ward 13, Savin Hill	59.6	63.9	53.8
Ward 12, Roxbury*	59.2	65.6	50.1
Ward 15, Dorchester	57.3	61.3	46.8
Ward 22, Brighton	55.0	57.9	53.1
Ward 11, Jamaica Plain, Roxbury*	52.2	56.0	49.4
Ward 3, North End, West End, South End	51.7	56.6	49.5
Ward 10, Jamaica Plain	51.2	55.6	47.1
Ward 9, Roxbury, South End*	50.2	50.2	51.0
Ward 14, Dorchester, Mattapan*	48.6	54.1	41.3
Ward 8, Roxbury, South End*	44.5	52.1	41.7
Ward 21, Allston	38.1	40.7	31.9
Ward 5, Beacon Hill, Back Bay	37.3	42.9	38.8
Ward 4, Back Bay, South End	30.9	35.1	27.9
Boston	60.0	61.0	62.0

Source: "Annual Report of the Election Department," Boston, Massachusetts (1977-1981).
*Wards 8, 9, 11, 12 and 14 represent the bulk of the black community in Boston.

disadvantage potential black voters. Note that the voter registration rates in all of the white working-class areas, as well as in most of the white middle-class areas, are located in the upper ranges. All areas with significant numbers of black or Latino residents are located in the lower range. The only white areas in the city located in the lower range are Allston, Beacon Hill, and the Back Bay. The latter two areas, however, have a greater number of black and Latino residents than do any of the white areas with a voter registration rate greater than 60%.[27] These areas also have been traditionally characterized by low rates of voter registration. This arrangement may change as a result of the massive voter registration effort conducted by Operation Big Vote and the Mel King for Mayor campaign in 1983; but again, the change is not through the efforts of city hall—it is in spite of the efforts of city hall.

When one notes that in New York City, with a population more than 11 times that of Boston, a voter registration system by mail has been implemented effectively, the procedures in Boston can be viewed as conveniently anachronistic.[28] Voter registration in Boston could be made relatively easy. This is not the case, in our view, because the mayor's machine has used voter registration procedures to control the number of blacks who are allowed to participate in the electoral arena. Encouraging this perception is the fact that very few blacks work in the Elections Department. In 1981 this city department employed 28 people, of whom only 2 were black.

Kimball has pointed out how voter registration procedures can create legal and psychological obstacles for minority potential voters when it is not in the interest of the entrenched to have new voters registered:

> It is imperative to focus on the institutional barriers that prevent increase in registration. . . . The staffing of registration points is usually under the control of local organizations who sometimes have special interest in excluding potential new voters who might threaten the distribution of power. In areas where residents speak a language other than English, the absence of bilingual materials and bilingual registration workers can be keenly felt by timid applicants. The frequency of registration dates, the hours when the public is accommodated, the availability of registration opportunities in locations other than central government offices—all have differential effects on the ability of some to register, particularly those with limited time off from work or limited access to transportation.[29]

Psychological obstacles are also created when unregistered potential voters are not encouraged actively to become participants in the electoral processes. Kimball argues that individuals must be made to feel that their participation is not only welcomed, but important. In his study of Newark he discovered, for example, that given

> ... two persons with similar disadvantages as to education, income, or race, the one who would register and vote displayed no self-evident differences from the neighbor who failed to participate. Although recency of arrival was sometimes a factor, mobility as such was not especially significant. Family backgrounds of participants or non-participants more or less washed out in the sample of unregistered surveyed in Newark. The key difference between voters and nonvoters seemed to be their own opinion of themselves, whether or not they felt they possessed the aptitudes for politics, whether or not they felt that the participation of one individual like themselves would make any difference.[30]

Those in power therefore have the capability of encouraging or discouraging voter registration and, generally, participation in a city's political processes.

Boston is a city where voter registration and turnout in the black community has been difficult or easy depending on the political needs of the mayor and his machine. Note the following tables. In 1967 Kevin White squeaked by Louise Day Hicks in the mayoral general election. If not for the black vote in wards 9, 12, and 14, White would have lost to Hicks by 426 votes. In the black community White swamped Hicks 15,569 to 3,202, thus beating her citywide 97,340 to 85,399. Because of this close election in 1967, as well as his poor showing among black voters in his 1970 gubernatorial bid, White aggressively wooed the black vote in 1971. In this year Robert A. Jordan, a black political columnist for the *Boston Globe,* reported that White's re-election campaign was intensively seeking a major portion of the more than 35,000 potential voters in the black community through black-oriented radio and newspaper advertisements, including some that suggested, "A vote for Atkins [a black mayoral candidate] is a vote for Hicks."[31]

Not coincidentally, a total of 8,000 new black voters were registered. Frieda Garcia, a longtime human service worker and community activist in Boston, explained how easy it was to register blacks and Latinos to vote during this period. The mayor made it possible for potential voters to be registered in their homes! Workers were

TABLE 7
VOTE RETURNS FOR PRELIMINARY MAYORAL ELECTIONS IN BOSTON AND WARDS 9, 12, AND 14, 1967-1979

Candidate and Year	Votes Cast in All Boston Wards Except Wards 9, 12, and 14	Votes Cast in Wards 9, 12, and 14	Total Vote
September 1967			
Kevin White	27,500	3,289	30,789
Louise Day Hicks	42,020	1,702	43,722
September 1971			
Kevin White	42,593	4,320	46,913
Louise Day Hicks	41,803	490	42,293
September 1975			
Kevin White	43,131	6,117	49,248
Joseph Timilty	37,931	1,066	38,997
September 1979			
Kevin White	47,291	3,053	50,272
Joseph Timilty	32,501	525	33,026
Melvin King	12,679	4,811	17,490

Source: "Annual Report of the Election Department," Boston, Massachusetts (1967-1980).

allowed to carry official registration rosters to various sectors in the black community. In fact, some even felt that White paid too much attention to the black community during this period. One observer wrote of an unspoken issue in the 1971 preliminary mayoral election: "There is the issue that no candidate talks about—the 'Mayor Black Phenomenon.' People in many areas of the city have felt, ever since he defeated Mrs. Hicks for mayor in 1967, that White funnels city resources into the black community at the expense of other neighborhoods."[32]

In the general election of 1971, White beat Hicks in the black community by 13,707 votes, but won the election by 40,873 votes. At this point he began to build a base in white working-class areas, forsaking the black community because during general elections, when he was challenged by candidates perceived to be anti-black,

TABLE 8
VOTE RETURNS FOR MAYORAL GENERAL ELECTIONS IN BOSTON AND WARDS 9, 12, AND 14, 1967-1979

Candidate and Year	Votes Cast in All Boston Wards Except Wards 9, 12, and 14	Votes Case in Wards 9, 12, and 14	Total Vote
November 1967			
Kevin White	79,470	15,569	95,039
Louise Day Hicks	86,879	3,202	90,081
November 1971			
Kevin White	98,581	14,556	113,137
Louise Day Hicks	69,482	849	70,331
November 1975			
Kevin White	71,307	9,751	81,058
Joseph Timilty	71,716	1,906	73,622
November 1979			
Kevin White	70,638	7,410	78,048
Joseph Timilty	61,374	2,895	64,269

Source: "Annual Report of the Election Department," Boston, Massachusetts (1967-1980).

that community did not have to be wooed. Under these circumstances, the registration of new black voters was no longer a priority of the city's political machine. When high voter registration in the black community has been advantageous to city hall, obstacles have been overcome in registering blacks; however, when it has been a disadvantage, blacks have received less encouragement to register.[33]

We have discussed a few institutional factors that have inhibited black people in Boston from greater levels of political participation in the electoral arena. Another major factor is the type of black political leadership that emerged in this city under Kevin White. Though black community leadership is diverse, the political machine in Boston attempted to prevent the emergence of a broad leadership group that might challenge the mayor's influence. The machine successfully established and legitimized its own black leadership by appointing "liaisons" to the black community. These liaisons were of two types, described in an earlier study of black politics by Wilson:

the "prestige" leader and the "token" leader. The former included those individuals who "invariably represent high—for the Negro community—personal achievement, achievement that usually flows from success in business or professional life."[34] These "prestige leaders are cited most often by other Negro leaders as having the 'best' or the most 'extensive' contacts with influential white leaders."[35] The other kind of liaison was the token leader,

> ... the Negro selected most often by whites, to "represent" the Negro community in civic activities and on public agencies where it is felt such representation is required. He lacks the status of the prestige leader, and the scope of his contacts with the white community tends to be narrower and more focused.[36]

These highly visible individuals were recruited by the political machine of Boston to positions lacking in substantive or institutionalized power. Part of this strategy was to make available to the black community a certain amount of patronage, controlled by city hall via these liaisons. This patronage was characterized not only by its relatively small amount, but also by its very nature. It was patronage that would not arouse concern on the part of white neighborhood groups. It might be a small grant from a public agency or a job for a loyal worker; it would not include, for instance, a reduction in property assessment for blacks in Roxbury, where rates are the highest in Boston. This latter type of patronage would require an equitable distribution of the property tax burden, which would mean that assessments of white homeowners would have to be increased. The relatively small amount of patronage made available to the black community was accepted as a given by the black liaisons.

This liaison system short-changed blacks even in terms of petty patronage by inhibiting the effectiveness of independent black leaders, who tended to demand greater amounts of patronage and systematic benefits. But by the creation of an artificial leadership for the black community and the appearance of access and influence through the careful use of limited patronage, city hall ensured that segments of the black community remained quiet and loyal. In this way, the machine attempted to convince blacks that independent political mobilization was not even necessary. This allowed city hall to maintain the political and economic arrangements that it had established with the white working class, as well as with more powerful groups in Boston.

The role of leadership is crucial for the political development of any black community in the American city; how leadership defines itself and is defined by external forces determines what issues will be generated and also affects the self-image of the black community. Without denying the importance of environmental factors, or the education and skills of black leaders, we would argue that the particular type of leadership is a crucial influence on the development and the level of political power. The significance of leadership for black political power is confined neither to Boston nor to the contemporary period.

In a study of blacks in Massachusetts at the turn of the century, Daniels claimed that the quality of leadership provided by prominent blacks determined the racial progress of the group.[37] And even earlier, black leaders in the ante-bellum period had developed extensive political and organizational expertise as a result of abolition committees, convention politics, and race-issues agitation; this experience, however, did not necessarily result in greater political sophistication—partly because of the role that leadership played:

> Negroes gained considerable experience in methods akin to those of politics, which subsequently gave them greater confidence in advancing their claims. After the war they of course expected to be of more political consequence. But whatever effort they exerted on their own behalf was of secondary importance and effect, for they were immediately made the proteges of white friends and enthusiasts, at whose hands they forthwith became recipients of bountiful patronage. During a period of twenty years at least, the outflowing favor of the other race was the factor in the appointment of Negroes to many respectable posts and in their election to the City Council and the State Legislature.[38]

Daniels describes specific instances illustrating this pattern and its consequences in the early 1900s: "Though four of the nine members of the Republican ward committee have usually been Negroes, they have obediently taken their orders from the white boss and have probably done more to injure their race in a political way than to help it." The author continues,

> The Negroes have failed dismally in this ward to realize their political opportunities. By 1905, the Negro males of voting age formed over 25%, and today they form close to 35%, of all the males of voting age in the ward. The white Republican males of voting age constitute a proportion of about 20% of the total. By enterprising registration of their own and the white Republican vote, and by taking advantage of factional quarrels among the Democrats, the Negroes could probably have obtained control of the ward and have elected members of their

race to the Common Council and to the Legislature. But whenever the better element have nominated a ward committee, as a first step in this direction, the Negro members of the regular "machine" committee have forthwith sown seeds of dissension... with the result that the "machine" has always won.[39]

A contemporary observer has also detected weaknesses in Boston's black leadership that have hurt the political advancement of black people:

> The dynamics of the black community have been enigmatic and unpredictable and often hard to see. Largely, the black sub-culture dynamics, particularly with regard to political behavior, have operated in a reactive manner; these dynamics have seldom been asserted through a political logic of their own but have been more inclined to respond to movements—shifts of power—within wider (white) societal structures. This has had the predictable but nonetheless detrimental effect of advancing a few—those closest to the centers of power—beyond the confines of the sub-culture at the expense of the rest.[40]

The patterns outlined here are still prevalent today. Sectors within the black leadership spectrum have not developed independently, but as scions of white power structures. The consequences of this type of leadership for the black community are remarkably similar to those observed in the early 1900s.

In Boston the black leadership established by the mayor's office between 1967 and 1983 inhibited the political growth of the black community and discouraged the development of progressive electoral activism. Until the black community in Boston asserts its independence and challenges the distribution of wealth and the particular arrangement of power, it will not enjoy political power. A significant step in this direction occurred in the September 1983 mayoral preliminary election, when Mel King received close to 95% of the black vote.

The appointed black officials who act as if they are in fact leaders in the traditional sense slow this potential development. One prominent educator in the black community described the following scenario when asked how the interests of the black community are expressed under a system of appointed black leaders: "A group of blacks will come together to discuss an important problem and then seek out someone who may have a personal contact with someone in the mayor's office; this person will then be asked to petition the mayor or some public bureaucrat for the favor of satisfying the request." This type of relationship is not based on power or the threat of power but on the benevolence of city hall's machine. This is an accurate description of the traditional "gate-keeper" role assigned to some black leaders by white power structures in cities throughout American history.

In discussing early black leadership in New York City, Katznelson described the relationship between city hall and the black community: "A black leader, handpicked by the white-controlled machine, delivered votes while avoiding contact with white voters in the area. In return, the leader achieved prestige because of this influence with his white patrons, and personal privilege.... The black voters which the leader mobilized were awarded a few menial patronage jobs to create an illusion of progress."[41] These black leaders, argues Katznelson, were not "representative in that territorial community procedures for leadership selection were absent. The black leaders were chosen by the white party elites, not by the community—territorial or racial—they claimed to represent."[42] These leaders were not "of" the black community, and therefore their positions were dependent on the good will of those whites on the top:

> These liaison or buffer leaders were given a taste of honey, the illusion of political access and some visible patronage. But these political rewards, they knew, came not as the product of independently organized territorial control, but from the white party leadership. The result, of course, was to detach the recognized black leaders from the mass of the black population. If position, for the black leadership, rested not on a mass base from below but was conferred from above, then what was conferred could always be retracted."[43]

Various sociological studies of black communities in the 1950s also help to describe the weaknesses of "non-institutionalized" leadership:

> Although there is an identifiable structure of leadership in the subcommunity of Pacific City at the present time, the leaders themselves are not "power wielders" or "decision makers" in the sense in which the terms are used by Hunter and Mills; they hold positions of little importance to the community's institutional structures; their decisions have no serious ramifications for the larger community.[44]

These same weaknesses are evident today with part of the black leadership stratum in Boston. Black leadership supported by city hall and white power structures was used effectively to slow the momentum that Mel King was developing in the black community during the mayoral preliminary campaign in 1979. Appointed black leaders have also been used to provide electoral support for white candidates such as Louise Day Hicks, recognized as being an "anti-black" politician by the black community.[45]

In addition, this artificial leadership has presented obstacles to the development of genuine black leadership. Former state Senator Bill Owens has said that he first decided to run for office because this type of leadership was hurting the black community by not allowing potential black leaders to exercise options for growth. He stated that a few political families in the black community have been nurtured as "gate-keepers" in order to maintain the political, economic, and social status quo. Representatives of these families have established political and economic structures that are specifically used to dampen the growth of black political independence. Owens explained, "If you look at organizations with positive intentions that have failed to get off the ground since the early sixties you will find the same names associated with them; the same people over and over again have been responsible for black political failures."[46] At times "organizations" without any structure are established to discourage independent action. In return for their services to the various white power structures, black "influentials" remain in what they consider to be prestigious positions, and accrue some minimal individual economic benefits. Remaining aloof from various efforts to mobilize the black community politically, these appointed black leaders have not addressed public issues in ways that might be disfavored by city hall. Liaison leaders are used as "lightning rods" to "cool out" angry blacks,[47] serving as buffers between the black community and city hall. They have been noticeably absent in electoral activities discouraged by city hall. An example was the lack of active involvement by liaison leaders in voter registration efforts during the 1979 preliminary election, when black voter registration would have been detrimental to Kevin White because of the presence of a black mayoral candidate.

Black liaison leaders have been used by white power structures to dampen the political aggressiveness of the black community. These anointed black leaders do not have institutionalized access to city hall or to the powerful interests operating in Boston; they serve not at the pleasure of their constituents, but at the pleasure of the mayor. Black leaders who are sanctioned by city hall are allowed to distribute small amounts of patronage in order to maintain the loyalty of black voters, but they cannot represent the interests of the black community. Their function is rather to explain or rationalize city hall's political behavior and policy to the black community. Black political mobilization is thus redirected from targeting city hall onto these individual leaders who are powerless to respond to the needs of the black community.

Black communities in American cities are beginning to reflect an electoral activism that rejects leadership by the mere appointees of the powerful—whether black or white. Blacks are realizing that change can only be a result of direct challenges to power; for this to occur, "propped-up" black leaders, such as those supported by the liaison system in Boston, must be replaced with leaders who are progressive and independent.

Another segment of black leadership in Boston includes individuals associated with the human services bureaucracies, specifically the "anti-poverty" structures. The relationship between this sector and the mayor's machine has been complex. Unlike other major cities, where anti-poverty structures have made an impact on the political development of black and Latino communities by providing resources to emerging political leaders of color, the impact of these structures in Boston has been limited.[48] Action for Boston Community Development, Inc. (ABCD), the city's umbrella anti-poverty structure, has had a mixed and sometimes stormy relationship with city hall but has not attempted to exercise power or influence in the local electoral arena. This organization has restricted its major role to that of a pressure group, periodically becoming activated around issues that directly affect the organization's delivery of services and its clients. This has led the organization to be more state- than city-oriented in the electoral arena, a posture not consistent with ABCD's history in Boston. Thernstrom reported that the agency's structure "was carefully designed to mirror the leadership structure of the community itself."[49] Initially this meant control of the agency by the business elite, but by the late 1960s the elite was replaced by city hall.[50] A third phase, during which city hall's influence declined, was only possible with the tacit understanding that ABCD would not seek to politically mobilize the black or poor citizens of Boston.

ABCD's apparently neutral role in city electoral activities has had a cost—discouraging the politicization of blacks in Boston. It has dampened the thrust for black political mobilization and inhibited the development of black leadership. Many neigborhood activists, recruited into ABCD, are in effect discouraged from participation in the city's political processes. This is similar to Hamilton's findings concerning the effect of anti-poverty structures on the institutionalization of political power in New York City's black and Puerto Rican communities. He found that while "participation in poverty-programs politics has increased in black communities, the level of political influence in the electoral arena has decreased."[51] In New York, Hamilton writes,

> The black constituency has lost, not gained, political influence, if one measures this in terms of the capacity to elect and influence people who will likely have control over the way programs are run. The black constituency has evidenced a marked decline in participation in the process (electoral politics) aimed at capturing and controlling not funded programs, but positions of governmental (institutional) power. This is the function of a politicization process gone awry.[52]

Hamilton focuses on the development of "recipients" as contrasted to "clients" as the key to an understanding of how anti-poverty programs have discouraged the institutionalization of black political power. As he argues, "A patron-recipient relationship is a political benefit structure that does not require the recipient to reciprocate in any sustained political way in order to receive benefits."[53] This discourages an electorally focused political socialization.

ABCD presents an additional "discouraging" dimension not discussed fully by Hamilton. This organization also minimizes the development of institutionalized power by depleting the number and energy of individuals who would tend to be attracted to electoral politics. Here we refer to those who are aware of the importance of local electoral activity but have been burdened with professional responsibilities associated with social services distribution. Their work orientation diverts political interests to human service and bureaucratic matters. For example, a number of individuals in ABCD, previously active in local politics, were co-opted into the delivery of human services and excluded themselves from electoral politics. But as Hamilton writes, "The leaders and spokespersons of such a constituency are at a distinct disadvantage in the pluralist bargaining process. They must attempt to function in the competitive political industry with less than adequate resources. They are rendered weak by the nature of their own benefit support system."[54] Potentially influential community leaders are rendered harmless in the electoral arena by ABCD.

In addition to ABCD, there is another layer of programs, either linked to ABCD as local neighborhood offices or supported by private funds. In contrast to ABCD personnel, leaders in this sector have been more active electorally. For example, some supported and actively campaigned for Mel King in the preliminary mayoral elections of 1979 and 1983. These leaders are issue-conscious and sensitive to the linkage between the services their clients receive, various kinds of community problems, and the electoral development of the black community.

Generally, however, city hall used its influence to discourage political independence based on black-managed anti-poverty structures. This was done by allowing some blacks a relatively free hand in administering local poverty funds. An understanding was reached between city hall and these administrators that those who were not a threat to the political machine would be rewarded, in part, by being allowed to use poverty monies as they saw fit—as long as it was done within the legal guidelines of specific programs.

One writer commented that this system of electoral control is similar to that used by Mayor Joseph Alioto in San Francisco: "Both White and Alioto employed Model Cities, OEO, job programs, and similar federal patronage resources to sustain minority community support while acting tough on disorder and boosting growth. They employed their federal resources all the more shrewdly by allowing 'community control,' rather than exercising tight oversight over funds and employees. But they knew when to call in their debts."[55]

Even in Chicago, a powerful political machine had to allow a "certain semblance of participation" in controlling anti-poverty funds. Greenstone and Peterson found that:

> However efficiently the Neighborhood Service Center (NSC) was operated, among the purposes which it studiously avoided fulfilling was the political activation of low income groups. The Daley Administration was uninterested in spawning political competitors, and it had the political resources and bureaucratic apparatus sufficient to prevent CAP encouragement of such developments. A certain semblance of participation was a necessary concession to OEO, but the clear preference and actual accomplishment of Chicago's CAA was to keep it at the minimum feasible level.[56]

Mayor White influenced the direction of Boston anti-poverty funds in this same way. In contrast, the mayor of Philadelphia encouraged the politicization of the anti-poverty programs to fight established interests. Here, Bailey found, "Politics is very much a part of the city's war on poverty.... The mayor has used the anti-poverty program to gain political support in his fight with the city's Democratic Party chairman. Anti-poverty workers were perceived to work for the mayor's re-election to office."[57] In Boston, White controlled the political machine thoroughly. He did not necessary need anti-poverty programs to keep him in control of his machine. The White strategy was based on neutralizing this potential political resource.

When this strategy was not effective, the White machine directly challenged uncooperative anti-poverty program leaders. For example, in 1972, the Model Cities Program—under the mayor's control—was used against uncooperative individuals in one anti-poverty program, the Roxbury Action Program (RAP). Paul Parks, the Model Cities administrator appointed by White, was directed by city hall to challenge public funding to RAP for the development of a housing project in Kittredge Square in Roxbury, an area virtually ignored by city hall until RAP expressed an interest in it. In a related development, White also used Parks in his position as Housing Commissioner to hold up approval of the Boston Housing Authority's sale of its property to RAP. State Representative Doris Bunte, who was aligned with RAP and a member of the Boston Housing Authority, was dismissed by White. In a study of this incident, Perry writes, "Part of this campaign included foot-dragging by White administration officials in other city departments on actions necessary to the work of the BHA Board."[58] In response to these attempts to control and coerce RAP, the organization attempted (though unsuccessfully) to run a slate on the Boston Model Neighborhood Board in 1969 and 1970. By co-opting some black anti-poverty program leaders and forcing others onto the defensive, the White machine used the anti-poverty funds to help maintain the arrangement of power relationships in the city or, at the minimum, to neutralize these programs as potential sources of political challenge to his regime.

White and his personal machine used the political resources described here to depress the level of black participation in the electoral arena, and to discourage a progressive politics that would seriously threaten business as usual in Boston. The sometimes subtle, but effective political obstacles that big-city mayors place before growing and aware black communities will become more obvious as blacks

82   FROM ACCESS TO POWER

grope for power, rather than accommodation. As independent black leaders seek to challenge the political and economic status quo, city hall impediments will have to be removed or eliminated. We will next show how the Mel King campaigns in 1979 and 1983 sought to do this.

Notes

1. Bertram M. Gross and Jeffrey F. Kraus, "The Political Machine Is Alive and Well," *Social Policy* (Winter 1982), p. 38.
2. *Ibid.*, p. 41.
3. Jack Newfield and Paul Dubrul, *The Permanent Government: Who Really Runs New York*, The Pilgrim Press, New York, 1981, p. 63.
4. Edward Greer, *Big Steel: Black Politics and Corporate Power in Gary, Indiana*, Monthly Review Press, New York, 1979, p. 12.
5. *Ibid.*, p. 13.
6. William E. Nelson, Jr. and Philip J. Meranto, "Electing Black Mayors," *Political Action In Black Campaigns*, Ohio State University Press, 1977, p. 23.
7. Gross and Kraus, *op. cit.*, p. 44.
8. *Ibid.*, p. 46.
9. *Ibid.*
10. For a discussion of this point, see "The Bankers Take Over," in Newfield and Dubrul, *op. cit.*
11. See *In These Times:* "Chicago Blacks Test Independence" (June 16, 1982), "Brooklyn Blacks Fight City Hall" (May 25, 1982), and "Revenge of the Good Ole Boys" (Jan. 20, 1982).
12. Interestingly, a few observers have argued that a political machine does not exist in this city; Eric Nordlinger in *How the People See Their City*, MIT Press, Cambridge, Mass., 1972, claims that "Boston does not have a machine, or anything remotely resembling one. Even James Michael Curley's machine was largely a loyal personal following rather than a powerful political organization, as widely believed. Curley, who lost more mayoral elections than he won, left behind a machine too fragile to be passed on to a successor after his death despite the absence of an internal feud over the succession." But seemingly contradictory to this is his observation that the mayor's "Little City Halls" project was easily used to maintain his political organization:

> Many ... OPS (Office of Public Services) staff worked on the mayoral campaign. At least three-quarters did so; and to a far greater extent than in the gubernatorial campaign. The work was done on the city's time. Staff persons in secretarial and administrative positions collected, organized and typed up lists of potential supporters and campaign workers; staff members sent out direct mailings and worked as interviewers on public opinion surveys; managers and high level administra-

tors in OPS central worked closely with the Mayor's office and campaign staff on a wide range of activities. (p. 87)

Kevin White's political machine may have been his own, and did not reflect the style of previous powerful urban machines; but the essential features were present. The White machine could organize between 2,000 and 3,000 workers for any city election, as was done in the 1979 mayoral campaign (*Boston Globe*, September 7, 1979, and *Boston Ledger*, February 29, 1980). White's machine was even able to provide Louise Day Hicks, a staunch anti-busing leader perceived as anti-black, with black city employees to assist her in an election bid to the City Council. The White machine suffered a few setbacks; in 1981 only one of its seven endorsed City Council candidates won election to this body, for example. The mayor frequently found himself at odds with a number of state legislators in Boston. But all of this only meant that the White machine was not perfect. Until White's announcement that he would not seek a fifth term, it was the most organized and consistent political force in Boston. See the following for standard descriptions of a political machine: Raymond Wolfinger, *The Politics of Progress*, Prentice-Hall, Inc., New Jersey, 1974, p. 99; and Hanes Walton, *Black Politics: A Theoretical and Structural Analysis* (Philadelphia: Lippincott Co., 1972), p. 56.

13. Newfield and Dubrul, *op. cit.*, p. 279.

14. Chuck Stone, *Black Political Power in America*, Bobs Merrill Co., New York, 1967, p. 81.

15. *Boston Phoenix* (November 6, 1979).

16. Peter Bachrach and Morton Baratz, *Power and Poverty: Theory and Practice*, Oxford University Press, New York, 1970.

17. *Ibid.*, p. 43.

18. *Ibid.*, p. 44.

19. William Albersts, *The 'White' Magic of Systemic Racism*, Billeva Press, Boston, MA., 1977, p. 2.

20. *Boston Globe* (June 13, 1982).

21. Nicholas Danigelis, "Black Political Participation in the United States: Some Recent Evidence," *American Sociological Review* (October 1978), p. 757.

22. *Ibid.*, p. 760.

23. The mayor proposed similar reforms in 1977, but much suspicion about his motivation was generated; black and white groups accused him of political opportunism. State Representative Thomas M. Finneran (15th Suffolk District, Mattapan) expressed the reasons for this: "It is no secret that Kevin White has advocated charter reform only when it would further his own political goals and machinations.... Faced with [sic] a vigorous and independent council, White is now pushing for 'reform' again. Those of us in the local political arena are quite familiar with the power of the mayor's machine. It is well-oiled, fueled by illegal patronage and in a commanding position to seize every single one of the district-level council positions" (*Boston Globe*, July 28, 1980). The reform thrust of 1977 was also open to suspicion from certain white sections of Boston. The *Boston Globe* reported around this time that

"Just below the surface of the low-key debate, however, is a concern with white voters in such neighborhoods as South Boston, Charlestown, West Roxbury, Hyde Park and much of Dorchester that they will consider the referendums the 'black question' and vote no to increasing black political influence on those bodies" (*Boston Globe*, Nov. 2. 1977).

24. *Latino Political Action Committee, et al. v. City of Boston, et al.*, 1982.

25. *Campaign for District Representation, Boston Tenant Organization, District 40 Community Education and Social Agency Employees, and Boston People's organization v. Kevin White*, 1982.

26. See Section 24, Chapter 3 of Revised Ordinances and Chapter 236 of the Acts of 1966.

27. See "The Racial Composition of Boston's Neighborhoods: 1980" in *Characteristics of Boston's Population and Housing, 1980, op. cit.*, p. A-1.

28. In New York City, too, voter registration sometimes has been used as a political resource. In an interview with Professor Arthur Klebanoff concerning the significance of poverty, apathy, and fear as an explanation for the low rate of voter registration among blacks and Puerto Ricans, the *New York Times* was given the following response: "All those factors were at work, and more so all through the South. The truth is that the political leadership in this town doesn't want more registered voters, because they prefer small, controllable constituencies. Even the black district leaders face this—they want to be able to beat insurgents, and if they let the rolls increase with all these strange voters, they'll lose control of the process" (*New York Times*, January 13, 1974).

29. Penn Kimball, *The Disconnected*, Columbia University Press, New York, 1972, p. 297.

30. *Ibid.*, p. 295.

31. *Boston Globe* (September 11, 1971).

32. *Boston Globe* (September 8, 1971).

33. Conceivably, it could be argued that the discrepancies between the voter registration rates of white and black neighborhoods reflect socioeconomic differences; in other words, poorer areas would not exhibit the level of voter registration found in better-off areas. If this were the case, however, the gap between white working-class neighborhoods and the black community should not be as large as it is. In addition to this, it has also been discovered that black political characteristics are not as influenced by social and economic attributes as are white political characteristics. This is generally true of urban communities in the North and the South. One early study discovered that, "The level of Negro voter registration in Southern counties is far less a matter of the attributes of the Negro population than of the white population and of the community:" Donald Matthews and James Protho, "Social and Economic Factors in Negro Voter Registration in the South," *The American Political Science Review* (March 1963), p. 34. This study concluded that "the personal attributes of Negroes—their occupations, income, and education as reflected in county figures—were found to have relatively little to do with Negro registration rates" (p. 41). In *Participation in America*, Harper & Row,

New York, 1972, Sydney Verba and Norman Nie report that when socioeconomic status is controlled, blacks participate in the electoral processes to a greater extent than whites. They discovered that based on the socioeconomic levels they used, "At five out of six socioeconomic levels blacks participate more than whites" (p. 156). They continue, "Rather than the average black being an under-participator, we find that he participates in politics somewhat more than we would expect given his level of education, income, and occupation, and more than the white of similar status" (p. 157). Considering this, it would seem that white working-class areas should not be expected to have voter registration rates much greater than the rates found in black neighborhoods. This all suggests that relatively poor white areas should not have a voter registration rate of 22 to 25 percentage points higher than the average rate for the black community (50.7%) unless there is some "intervening" explanation. The way in which voter registration was approached by City Hall is such an intervening variable.

34. James Q. Wilson, *Negro Politics: The Search for Leadership*, The Free Press, Glencoe, Ill., 1960.
35. *Ibid.*, p. 257.
36. *Ibid.*, p. 261.
37. John Daniels, *In Freedom's Birthplace*, Arno Press, New York, 1914, p. 292.
38. *Ibid.*, p. 268.
39. *Ibid.*, p. 282.
40. Charles J. Hamilton, Jr., "Changing Patterns of Negro Leadership in Boston" (unpublished honors thesis, Harvard University, 1969), p. 8.
41. Ira Katznelson, *Black Men, White Cities*, Oxford University Press, New York, 1973, p. 68.
42. *Ibid.*, p. 118.
43. *Ibid.*, p. 84.
44. Ernest A.T. Barth and Baha Abu-Laban, "Power Structure and the Negro Sub-Community," *American Sociological Review* 24 (February 1959), p. 75.
45. *Boston Globe* (November 30, 1979).
46. Interview with state Senator Bill Owens, June 15, 1980.
47. This term is borrowed from Wilbur C. Rich, "Special Role and Role Expectation of Black Administrators of Neighborhood Mental Health Programs," *Journal of Community Mental Health* 2, 10 (1975).
48. For one excellent discussion of the relationship between anti-poverty structures and their impact on politics in five cities, see David Greenstone and Paul Peterson, *Race and Authority in Urban Politics*, Russell Sage Foundation, New York, 1973.
49. Stephen Thernstrom, *Poverty, Planning, and Politics in the New Boston: The Origins of ABCD*, Basic Books, Inc., New York, 1969, p. 163.
50. *Ibid.*, p. 190.
51. Charles V. Hamilton, "The Patron-Recipient Relationship and Minority Politics in New York City," *Politics Science Quarterly* (Summer 1979), p. 21.

52. *Ibid.*, p. 224.
53. *Ibid.*, p. 225.
54. *Ibid.*
55. John Mollenkopf, "The Post-War Politics of Urban Development," *Politics and Society* 5,3 (1975), p. 228.
56. Greenstone and Peterson, *op. cit.*, p. 24.
57. Harry A. Bailey, Jr., "Poverty Politics and Administration: The Philadelphia Experience," in Miriam Ershkowitz and Joseph Zikmund II (eds.), *Black Politics in Philadelphia*, Basic Books, New York, 1973, p. 184.
58. Stewart E. Perry, *Building a Model Black Community: The Roxbury Action Progam*, (Center for Community Economic Development, Cambridge, MA), p. 57.

PART TWO
The Mel King for Mayor Campaigns, 1979 and 1983

V

Boston: Chaos or Community?

Mel King and James Jennings

> The stability of the large world house which is ours will involve a revolution of values to accompany the scientific and freedom revolutions engulfing the earth. We must rapidly begin to shift from a thing-oriented society to a person-oriented society. When machines and computers, profit motives and property rights are considered more important than people, the giant triplets of racism, materialism and militarism are incapable of being conquered. A civilization can flounder as readily in the face of moral and spiritual bankruptcy as it can through financial bankruptcy.[1]

The Brookings Institution recently published a survey of American cities which attempted to rate the quality of urban life; Boston was rated at the lower end of the scale.[2] At one local conference where this report was discussed, many business and academic leaders criticized the study because of conceptual weaknesses.[3] There were some civic and political representatives who also argued against the findings of the report by claiming that Boston, contrary to the study's conclusions, is quite healthy both in terms of its sociopolitical character and its economy. This status, they argue, places Boston quite high in the rankings of quality of life among American cities. This reaction is interesting, for how can a city be healthy when a significant percentage of its residents feel that they are headed more toward chaos than community? Boston healthy? If racism and racial violence in this city are to be resolved, we must start by recognizing the ugly, unhealthy face of Boston.

Recently, the economist Lester Thurow lamented that our political system is not very efficient for solving the kinds of economic and social problems contributing to urban decline. But, ironically,

Our economic problems are soluble. For most of our problems there are several solutions. But all these solutions have the characteristic that someone must suffer large economic losses. No one wants to volunteer for this role, and we have a political process that is incapable of forcing anyone to shoulder this burden.[4]

In another recent work, two sociologists have argued that our problems can be tackled effectively—they suggest that whether we do, or not, may be more a question of moral fortitude than depressing econometric forecasting. As Blackwell and Hart write,

The nation cannot afford to turn its back on any of its citizens, irrespective of race, color, religion, or national origin. We still have time to continue to make progress toward equality of opportunity and racial justice. *Do we have the resolve?* Can it again become a national priority? Those are the central questions in the 1980s.[5]

We are in agreement with these ideas. To us these statements suggest that Boston does not have to grow and develop on the backs of its poor and working-class residents. We understand that economic development is a vital concern for our survival; but we also believe that it can be approached in a more balanced way than is presently the case. We are confident that Boston's social and economic ills—major contributors to the problem of racial violence—can be resolved without ignoring the needs of the poor, the elderly, minorities, and other disadvantaged groups.

Before his death, Martin Luther King, Jr., made a number of useful policy suggestions that we should consider today; these were discussed in his last major work, *Where Do We Go from Here?* It is important to remember, however, that his message was in two parts. In addition to specific policy suggestions, Martin Luther King, Jr., also delineated a *moral framework* by which we could develop a healthy city. It is our contention that King's moral message was as important as were his policy suggestions. Our social and economic problems cannot be solved without the moral thrust reflected in Martin Luther King's life and death. It is moral fortitude that will allow us to be creative and innovative in confronting the problems that separate us. Martin Luther King, Jr., and many others have provided the visions by which we can build cities livable for everyone. If our political policies are not intertwined with the moral thrust described by King in *Where Do We Go from Here*, we could very easily witness the speedy snapping of delicate social bonds. Along this line of thought, a new book by

Amitai Etzioni seems to be suggesting that the "ego-centered mentality" is destroying important institutions in America—such as the family—which mediate between the individual and the state.[6] Attention to this problem does not negate the need for effective technical and managerial approaches to our urban problems; but we also must develop the values that will allow us to see each other as fellow human beings.

In the next few pages we will try to describe the kinds of values that will allow us to tackle racial violence in Boston. We also hope to provoke some thought about how certain values might be used to develop a people-oriented public agenda that can eliminate racism, and all the other negative "isms" in our Boston.

We must develop a broad vision of the kind of city we want. We must, in the words of Kenneth Clark, "teach people how to help each other, to respect each other, and to respect the commonality inherent among all human beings," because "the continuing training of the human mind without regard to moral sensitivity" is the greatest danger facing the human species.[7] We must try to bring people together in order to define the basic values and issues that must underlie every effort we undertake, and also to nurture the vision of where we want to be, so that every individual and every group can see clearly how their participation may contribute to a Boston that is truly a home for everyone who lives in it, regardless of race, ethnicity, class, or religion.

In order to do this, progressive forces must use all tools at their disposal. We must use community forums, the courts, the public schools, and most definitely the "streets." We are not spiritual leaders; we cannot talk of saving souls. But our experiences, both in the practice and study of politics, lead us to believe that all progressive efforts must be ingrained with certain moral values. A progressive politics must be developed at the same time that certain people-oriented values are nurtured; one cannot occur without the other. The Boston Covenant has not succeeded. It tried to introduce morality without politics; conversely, a politics without morality will also be doomed to failure.

Perhaps the most important value to introduce as an underlying basis for the development of a progressive politics is *compassion*. This means that people, no matter what their race, ethnicity, or religion, empathize with the needs of other people. A compassionate person knows that so long as one human being is hungry while others are not, so long as one human being is cold while others are not, so long as some have and many do not have, humanity is diminished. A compassionate person feels compelled to respond to anything, any individual, or any institution that diminishes—whether intentionally or unintentionally—the human spirit. Compassion leads to *sharing*.

Sharing is crucial for the survival of urban America; this was a major finding of the President's Commission on Neighborhoods in a report issued in 1980.[8] Unless those who have begin to share with those who do not, America may experience tensions from which it may not be able to recover. As Martin Luther King, Jr., argued, wealth must be shared; decent housing must be shared; opportunities for the pursuit of happiness must be shared. We live in a society that has become the most powerful nation in the history of human kind. We are citizens of the richest nation in the world. But these riches and this power were attained through the exploitation of masses of people on the bottom; American world power was based upon a system that kept millions of black people enslaved for approximately two hundred and fifty years. And even after "emancipation" blacks were not allowed to participate fully in the affairs of their nation. In the name of profit, blacks and other people of color were kept on the bottom, and working-class whites were given a bit more breathing space for their complicity in the unscrupulous pursuit of profits. And what do we have as a result of this? We have ethnic and racial animosity, mistrust of each other, despair, and alienation. And still our economic problems have not been solved. The power—and spiritual beauty—of sharing, of people freely offering to each other what they have, is that we will be able to accomplish more, with less, if resources and skills are pooled. We must nurture our interdependence, and abandon the idea that every person can make it on his or her own. Only when we build processes based on inclusion will we be able to live together, and without racial or social violence in our midst.

Respect is an integral part of compassion and sharing. Respect means that we do not violate the physical and spiritual forces that are part of us. It means that we respect different ways of doing things, of learning, of living, and even of dying. It also means that we revere our earth. It is vital to our survival that we return to respecting our natural resources and the incredibly complex natural systems that we continue to abuse. We must respect the fact that our technology is only as good as we make it; the ultimate responsibility for its consequences falls on each of us, whether inventor, operator, or bystander. We must respect each other: each person has to be seen as a potential component of our whole community. We must stand together and challenge any robbery, murder, manipulation, bullying, or, worst of all, indifference in our communities.

Boston, and indeed all of urban America, must also nurture *creativity*. This means that people in all walks of life are encouraged to use their skills and talents to solve problems rather than to make money or to beat someone else out. In many ways society encourages people to make money as the only way to solve their problems. We must try to reverse this in certain situations; the emphasis should be on solving problems, not on making and spending money. For instance, how can wasted resources—such as our youth and elderly—be tapped to help solve the tensions of urban life? There are probably many young and old people who would be willing and able "to help out," not for monetary gain but for other kinds of gains. Can our youth be used to help and care for the elderly? And can our elderly be used to help educate our youth? Creativity and innovation may provide answers that are not only beneficial for everyone, but also relatively inexpensive.

An important value underlying the emerging progressive struggle in cities like Boston is the desire to create a sense of *community* for all people. By *community* we mean to suggest the social, economic, and cultural context in which people can live and feel nurtured, sustained, involved, and stimulated. Yes, this is vague—but it is also real. Community is the continual process of getting to know people, caring and taking responsibility for the physical and spiritual condition of urban living space.

Creating and maintaining a sense of community is the best way to meet people's needs. People relate better and more completely in a community. Working with their neighbors, people can accomplish an amazing amount not possible under an impersonal government program. We need to make use of the person next door and not depend on people outside the community to solve our problems and satisfy our needs. People flourish in a more personal environment: their strengths can be cultivated and their weaknesses can be improved with the support of neighbors with complementary sets of skills and strengths. Community counteracts the frustration, depersonalization, and fragmentation that our society forces on people.

Community is important for establishing a common bond across our city, for creating a sense of identity, for maintaining and creating cultural continuity, for giving social expression to oneself as a part of a larger whole, for developing an ever-widening sense of community, city, state, nation, and world.

Once we appreciate the importance of these values for urban survival, we can begin to incorporate them into the issues that affect the everyday lives of Bostonians. Urban issues should be identified and molded within strategic frameworks that encourage this kind of spiritual thrust.

Following are the broad parameters of a few problem areas Bostonians must grapple with if we are to make it to the twenty-first century as a community. In this limited space we cannot provide specific details about how these issues could be molded and implemented. We only wish to show how at a general level ideas like compassion, sharing, respect, and "sense of community" can be incorporated into a political agenda that engender racial peace in Boston. There are three areas that are especially crucial to all residents of the city: jobs, education, and housing.

JOBS

Public policymakers must approach the development of job opportunities as an immediate priority; this does not mean that we wait for some vague "trickle-down" process to provide the unemployed with jobs—we cannot afford to wait this long. Jobs must be created immediately. This can be encouraged on both the national and local levels. On the national level it means that our political representatives must agitate aggressively for the transfer of military dollars to greater job-producing sectors. Recently, for example, a local group, Jobs for Peace, found that for every one billion dollars the military spends in one year, 9,000 fewer jobs are created than if the same money were given to the private sector, and 35,000 fewer jobs are created than if it were given to state and local governments.[9]

At the local level there are a number of steps our government could pursue:

1. Enforce our jobs-residents ordinances; Boston residents should enjoy guaranteed access to private and public jobs in the city.
2. Encourage unions to open their doors more widely for the benefit of blacks, Latinos, and women.
3. Fund a comprehensive housing and energy development program that would provide jobs in neighborhoods, and save energy at the same time.
4. Encourage the business community to take a more active and aggressive posture toward the problem of youth unemployment. Tax policies should be used to reward socially-concerned businesses rather than those with just a passing interest in Boston. *We want businesses that can balance the social needs of the city with their pursuit of profits.*
5. Encourage suburban commuters to support policies and efforts that make our neighborhoods economically healthier.
6. Enforce affirmative action policies in the private and public sectors.

EDUCATION

General policy in this area should have two thrusts. First, it is clear that if the future requires us to work together cooperatively, then we all need to learn new skills relevant to coalition building, to conflict resolution, and to social problem solving. The community itself can undertake some of this education, as it has on a number of occasions when groups have shared their work and experience with others. But informal sharing is not all it will take.

The second element of education that is crucial to the survival of the city is the public school system. We have young people who have come up through schools not only unable to read and write, but also completely uninformed about the ways in which they could work on solving the problems of their neighborhoods. The lack of skills and information that relate to their own street experience, the lives of their families, and their own frustrations, and the feelings that are raised by the sight of dilapidated buildings, out-of-work people, and exposure to the anger generated by helplessness, guarantee that these kids will not be able to play constructive roles in their communities. They will be easy prey for destructive forces in our community that counteract all the good work being done. The schools have to change, and change drastically, in order to teach the building of strong and economically vibrant communities.

HOUSING

The city of Boston is facing a housing crisis; there is little decent and affordable housing for poor and working-class Bostonians. The massive displacement that was incorporated in redevelopment policies during the 1950s and 1960s has continued, and actually worsened during the current period. Despite neighborhood discontent and protest, profit- rather than people-oriented redevelopment practices continue. But where will the displaced, the poor, the working-class go? Can we just wish this problem away? Sadly, our local government has not only turned its back on those mired in the atrocities we call "public housing," it also continues to pamper interest groups that seem to have little concern for what happens to the people of Boston. Boston city government seems more a representative of high-powered builders from around the country than representatives of those who work, live, and die here. How can we talk honestly about solving the racial crisis in Boston when people are squeezed together like an overcrowded cage of rats? Making decent housing available to all is a guaranteed way of resolving the increasing racial violence in this city. Our government can take a number of important steps in this area by:

1. adopting strong rent control policies,
2. enforcing housing codes,
3. developing a community-controlled program of housing rehabilitation,
4. integrating the city's neighborhoods by enforcing civil rights legislation,
5. severely restricting the growth of condominium conversions,
6. restricting speculative real estate practices,
7. hiring youth to perform arson-prevention services, and
8. encouraging and organizing tenants to manage public housing.

These are steps that we can take now—and at very little additional cost.

CONCLUSION

Most of the land and buildings in Boston are owned and controlled by organizations and people based outside the city. While Boston is described as "a city of neighborhoods" made up of diverse ethnic groups, the fundamental reality is that the city is torn by racism and elitism. These problems—whether they are intentional or unintentional—are perpetuated by wealthy interests (and their managers) who see Boston not as a home, but as a source of lucrative investment returns. Ownership and control of land, housing, and factories have given a few people tremendous economic power and status. They have used this power to extract greater profits from Boston and its workers, its tenants, and its neighborhoods.

There has emerged—alongside those who control wealth and economic power—a considerable number of young professionals who have higher incomes and status than the working folks who live in the neighborhoods. Due to the increasing cost of commuting, and the appeal of the cultural diversity of the inner city, these young professionals are being herded into condominiums built by the realtors and banks; this, in turn, is forcing working folks, blacks, and Puerto Ricans out of their homes and neighborhoods. The war between the young professionals and the folks in the neighborhoods is one more chapter in the history of systematic attempts to maintain a segmented city so as to be able to further enrich some sectors at the expense of others.

This war can be prevented by decentralizing political power in Boston; political decentralization is necessary to allow people on the bottom to build a politics based on Martin Luther King, Jr.,'s moral thrust. We cannot continue to have a city government in which interests based outside Boston, and with little identification with our communities, can make indiscriminate decisions affecting how blacks, whites, and Latinos relate to each other. If the poor and working-class citizens of Boston are to be affected by various public (and private) policies, then decision and implementation input has to be broadened to include them. We feel that the more people are involved in the public arena, the more creative and effective the solutions are likely to be, and this does not preclude the services of those with special or technical skills. We suggest, however, that the technicians and managers must serve at the pleasure of our communities. Compassion, sharing, respect, and community are values that must temper our technocrats and their tools. Decentralized power will allow these values to nurture to a greater extent than will a political system that only the powerful find accessible.

People on the bottom, along with individuals who see the gravity of our problems, must move away from sterile politics. Those more interested in people than in profits must begin to assert themselves. The first step toward freedom is to start identifying oneself with the values and spirit described by Martin Luther King, Jr. We can overcome racism; we do have strength to make Boston a city livable for all its citizens. But we must begin to build a politics that will move away from "chaos," and carry us toward "community."

Notes

1. Martin Luther King, Jr., *Where Do We Go from Here: Chaos or Community?*, Beacon Press, Boston, 1967, p. 186.
2. C. Bradbury, A. Downs, and K. Small, *Urban Decline in American Cities*, Brookings Institution, Washington, 1982.
3. *The Cambridge Express*, December 17, 1982.
4. *The Zero-Sum Society*, Penguin Books, New York, 1982, p. x.
5. James E. Blackwell and Philip Hart, *Cities, Suburbs and Blacks*, General Hall, New York, 1982, p. x.
6. *An Immodest Agenda: Rebuilding America Before the 21st Century*, McGraw-Hill, New York, 1982.
7. *The Amsterdam News*, December 25, 1982.
8. "People Building Neighborhoods," *National Commission on Neighborhoods*, published by the Massachusetts Social and Economic Opportunity Council in Boston, March 1979.
9. *Jobs for Peace*, "Toward a Boston Peace Budget," October 1982, p. 24.

VI

The Making of Mel King's Rainbow Coalition: Political Changes in Boston, 1963-1983

James Green

On October 11, 1983 something electrifying happened in Boston. An inter-racial crowd jammed the Parker House and flowed out into the streets to celebrate a remarkable event in Boston's political history. Mel King, a militant black activist, a man of peace with feminist and socialist sympathies, had run a principled campaign for mayor, and stunned the city by winning a place in the run-off election. He finished in a dead heat with City Councilor Ray Flynn, formerly a state representative from South Boston. Characteristically, King led a demonstration from the Parker House down Tremont Street to City Hall Plaza where he gave an impromptu speech on what the place would be like when the people took over.

The press loved comparing the two finalists, "the craggy faced Irish battler from South Boston" and the "brawny, bald, bearded activist" from the South End. "The two men were the most leftward in the race, both running on a promise to shift money and urban planning energies away from glamorous downtown and harbor front development toward rebuilding Boston's neglected working-class neighborhoods." The two candidates' "populist appeals were so evenly matched" that *Time* magazine could not distinguish them.[1]

Indeed, each candidate did still live in the "rough Boston neighborhood where he was born and raised."[2] Both men had fathers who worked on the Boston docks and both attended public schools. Left unsaid was the fact that Mel King went to one of the city's few integrated schools, "the little United Nations" in the South End, while Ray Flynn starred in three sports at all-white South Boston High School. The two rough neighborhoods the candidates came from responded very differently to Boston's historic busing crisis. While white mobs stoned school buses full of black children in South Boston, parents in the South End formed escort groups for the white kids being bused into their schools. King and Flynn were both raised in poor, working-class neighborhoods, but more than the murky Fort Point Channel and the Amtrak yards separated the wide-open, multiracial South End from the all-white, intensely parochial neighborhood Ray Flynn had represented in the State House.[3]

Flynn and King had both declared their mayoral candidacies assuming that they would face Boston's incumbent, four-term mayor, Kevin White. As this article shows, White's administration was in crisis for many reasons, including the pressure of a federal corruption probe. When Mayor White decided not to run for a fifth term, the field opened up to include not only King and Flynn but also seven other candidates. Five were men of Irish or Italian background. There was one woman contender, the Socialist Workers Party candidate, who had trouble distinguishing herself from Mel King, and there was a provocative candidate from the crazy, right-wing U.S. Labor Party.

The front-runner in this field was David Finnegan, a slick talk-show host and former school committee chairman, who raised tons of money from downtown and suburban business interests, and inherited many of Kevin White's supporters. Flynn and King both aimed their attacks on Finnegan as the candidate of the rich who would carry on Kevin White's pro-business housing and development programs at the expense of the neighborhoods. This identification proved to be Finnegan's undoing, and he finished a poor third to King and Flynn, even though he outspent them by a vast margin. The preliminary election results were a repudiation of the pro-business "limousine liberalism" that had governed the city for decades. The election also recorded a major assertion of working-class discontent in both white and black communities. As a *Globe* columnist remarked: "The winners of the first post-White mayoralty preliminary are two candidates who weren't supposed to be there. Passion counted for more than money, ideology for more than TV ads. Populism beat charisma. And the media got shut out."[4]

However, Finnegan's defeat also had some troubling implications for the King campaign. If Mel had faced Finnegan in the final, he might have been able to win more white working-class votes from people hurt by the kind of economic and social policies that favored the downtown over the neighborhoods. But instead King faced Ray Flynn, who had carefully crafted his campaign, and indeed his recent political career, to appeal exactly to those white working-class voters hurt most by the pro-business policies of he White administration, and most offended by the arrogant, preppy style affected by both Mayor White and David Finnegan.

Mel King began his career in electoral politics in 1961 as a candidate for school committee and a dedicated enemy of racial segregation in schools and housing. Ray Flynn began his career as a South Boston politician in the heyday of Louise Day Hicks, the arch-segregationist, and built his career in the State House and on the city council as a "lunchbucket liberal" and a leading spokesman for anti-busing, anti-abortion forces. King attempted to make racism an issue in the mayoral campaign, and spoke out on the issue in a constructive way when he talked to audiences in all-white areas. Flynn insisted that racism was not an issue, but during the primary he passed out different leaflets in white and black areas. King identified himself as a feminist and spoke out against homophobia, while Flynn presented himself as a changed politician, a progressive who now opposed all sorts of discrimination. In recent years Flynn reversed his opposition on the Equal Rights Amendment and supported laws to prevent discrimination in housing based on race and sexual preference. But when he was asked how he would deal with violent attacks against women and gay men, Flynn simply said he would hire more police. And though he now claimed to support equal rights for women, Flynn did not renounce the amendment he sponsored in the State House to cut off Medicaid benefits for abortions to state employees and welfare recipients.

King and Flynn had different political histories, different principles and strategies, and as a result, they developed very distinctive grass-roots coalitions. Mel King's Rainbow Coalition developed out of the militant struggle against segregation waged by the black community and its white allies, a struggle which has come to include Asians and Latinos in the past decade. Because of King's active and principled opposition to all forms of discrimination, feminists, gays, and lesbians joined the coalition, as did most Boston area socialists who were impressed with Mel's leadership in a range of radical causes and by his ability to connect issues of discrimination, economic exploitation, imperialism, and militarism. All the leftists under the Rainbow also appreciated Mel King's courage, his willingness to maintain his principles and to fight back against race-baiting, red-baiting, and homophobia.

King's preliminary campaign had a decentralized, movement quality about it, somewhat reminiscent of the civil rights movement. And the candidate, who had declared his independence from the Democratic Party in 1977, enhanced this feeling by consistently referring to the "we" of the campaign and by looking beyond the elections to the long process of popular empowerment. Participation in the Rainbow Coalition eased many leftists' feelings of isolation and marginality. This foray into electoral politics offered us an unusual opportunity to transcend the limits of one-issue campaigns. We could work in a multi-national, multi-cultural coalition that brought together a range of issues and offered a progressive program we could take to ordinary people. For me and for many other white leftists campaigning in largely white working-class areas like Hyde Park, the effort allowed us to continue anti-racist political work in a new and more positive way. Mel King provided the leadership and encouragement we needed to take our politics to people in these conservative areas without being negative, defensive, or moralistic. Mel asked us to treat everyone as a "potential ally."

In his campaign Ray Flynn maintained his anti-busing, anti-abortion stance and took no chances on alienating his core constituency among conservative whites. He refused to recognize Boston's racist past or to use the term racism. He insisted the issues were the same in South Boston and in Roxbury. He turned his back on a historic opportunity to join Mel King and to address white people on the harmful effects of racism. He even refused to use his own immense influence in South Boston to intervene in the city council campaign in his home district between Jimmy Kelly, the ultra-right candidate of the anti-busing movement, and a liberal social worker.

Ray Flynn propelled himself into the final by distinguishing himself from the other white liberal democrats. He campaigned as a populist defending the little people in the neighborhoods against city hall and downtown business interests. At one point he confronted David Finnegan on City Hall Plaza declaring angrily, "This building is not for sale, David." Flynn understated and at times obfuscated his reactionary voting record on issues like busing and abortion. Of course, he already had the support of his conservative white, anti-busing, anti-abortion constituency. But this group would not be sufficient to make him a winner. Indeed, several single-issue anti-busing candidates had been defeated in the seventies. Flynn needed a broader base, including white liberal voters, and sought to widen his appeal by emphasizing his progressive record on economic issues, especially housing. As an at-large city councilor, Ray Flynn had assiduously cultivated union and community support throughout the city, visibly involving himself in supporting strikes, rent control campaigns, restrictions on condo conversion, while doing many political favors for individuals. While Flynn used his city council seat to cultivate citywide support, Mel King represented one district in the State House and tried to speak out on a wide range of issues concerning discrimination, exploitation, and militarism at home and abroad. While Flynn played a highly publicized role in the rent control struggle, King led the fight for a bill to divest the state of funds invested in South Africa. While the councilor from South Boston was doing favors for constituents, Mel King was doing that and more by taking leadership on larger issues that concerned people of color, visiting Cuba, and trying to bring together a black caucus of state legislators. King's record on economic issues was much more progressive than Flynn's. Indeed, it was King who developed two key proposals which Flynn later endorsed: the idea of linking neighborhood economic development to downtown growth and the Boston Jobs for Boston People program establishing quotas on public jobs for city residents, minorities, and women. But King lacked the visibility and credibility Flynn achieved in many neighborhoods around the city on very specific issues.

Mel King's preliminary campaign clearly represented empowerment for people of color. When King challenged incumbent Mayor Kevin White in the preliminary election of 1979, he finished third with 15 percent of the overall vote and 65 percent of the black vote. But in 1983 Mel nearly doubled his percentage of the total vote, swept the black community with 90 percent, and carried the Asian and Latino precincts with big majorities. His campaign and the idea of the Rainbow Coalition had dramatically boosted voter registration in minority areas with 23,000 new voters registering in the three weeks after his preliminary victory. King's 1979 mayoral campaign had seemed too radical for many black leaders, especially the ministers, but in 1983 national events altered the context for local politics and gave enormous impetus to progressive candidates like King. Harold Washington's historic victory in Chicago created new excitement and unity in Boston's black community. When Mayor Washington came to Boston in mid-summer to endorse King, his campaign surged forward in its recruitment and fund-raising activities. Visits by Andrew Young and Jesse Jackson added even more enthusiasm to the campaign and solidified King's black support. Soon the polls showed that Mel King had a chance to make the final run-off because most of the newly registered voters were people of color who planned to vote for him.

During the primary each candidate did make a populist appeal to the "poor, the near-poor and working class that felt left behind in Kevin White's glitzy downtown." And though both candidates did run similar campaigns on "ground-floor economic issues" like jobs and housing, there were some obvious differences.[5]

Though Flynn based his coalition on a traditional white anti-busing, anti-abortion constituency, he did attract significant liberal and social democratic support from some progressive leaders from groups like the Massachusetts Tenants Organization and Nine to Five. King of course had far more progressive support: from all of the women's groups and organizations representing people of color, from gay and lesbian activists, and from unions with significant minority membership and leftist leadership. But these defections to Flynn hurt. Progressive leaders like Lew Finfer of the Tenants Organization respected King but argued that Flynn had "done his homework" and used his position on the city council to be very visible on the issues and very helpful in doing favors. Other progressives and social democrats used a different kind of pragmatic argument: that a black candidate was not viable or electable in racist Boston and that it made more sense to back the best white progressive. Flynn's leftist supporters went beyond this, taking the incredible view of the liberal *Boston Globe* that their candidate showed a "greater willingness to reach out" than King, even though a miniscule number of people of color supported Flynn.[6] They also criticized Mel King for being ideological and divisive by injecting the issue of race into the campaign and thereby stirring up racism. And they tried to defend Flynn's terribly conservative record on race and women's issues, by emphasizing his economic populism and his recent support for some anti-discrimination laws. So when Flynn's supporters emphasized the "ground floor economic issues" and criticized King for raising the issue of racism and for allegedly acting like "the black candidate," they implied that race would not be a decisive factor in the final election.

But in the final election Boston did vote along racial lines. Flynn beat King by a two-to-one margin, carrying 80 percent of the white vote and only a small fraction of the vote cast by people of color. King's supporters naturally viewed this as a discouraging defeat. Blacks in the Rainbow Coalition had reason to be especially depressed. Once again white liberals had failed to support black people. Many did not vote and many others ignored Flynn's record of opposing desegregation, and decided to "back a winner." Though many white voters said they admired and respected Mel King personally, they refused to support him. Indeed, one discouraging poll showed that one-third of the white voters interviewed would not vote for a black candidate *under any circumstances*, no matter how appealing the candidate's proposals happened to be.[7]

Though naturally discouraged by the lack of white support, the King campaign did point out that Mel received 20 percent of the white vote, more than Harold Washington received in Chicago or Andrew Young in Atlanta, even though King ran a more radical campaign in a more overtly racist city. Many observers, as well as key black activists, thought that certain controversial statements alienated Catholics and cost King white votes. Others noted the gains Mel made in white areas over his 1979 campaign, even though he lacked a base in those areas and lacked the kind of support Flynn had developed in the unions and in the neighborhoods during his term as a city councillor. The people who took the King campaign into white neighborhoods had certainly hoped to do better, but they also thought they could win far more support the next time around if Mel King and the Rainbow Coalition could maintain visibility and activity in those areas.[8]

Though Mel King might have done better among white voters under different circumstances, he did not mourn his defeat on election night. After all, his campaign had empowered people of color in a very impressive way. The upsurge of voter registration among blacks, Asians, and Latinos was in itself an important achievement. The campaign had also forged a very vibrant coalition of people of color, women's groups, and white progressives that reoriented electoral politics in Boston. Though he had lost the race, King declared that the Rainbow Coalition had not been defeated. He thanked the crowd for allowing him to lead such a movement through "what historians will recognize as a turning point in the social, cultural and political history of Boston."[9]

Future struggles will be required to confirm this inspiring statement. But looking back over the past two decades of Boston politics, it is clear that the black struggle for equality has provided the leadership for an even broader movement for social tolerance and progressive change. The making of Mel King's Rainbow Coalition did not begin in 1983, but during that year the movement for economic, social, and cultural equality showed that it was ready to contest for political power. There have been some big changes in Boston politics since 1961, when Mel King first ran for the school committee in a campaign that, as he recalled, did not "excite any great interest."

In order to understand the changes that produced Mel King's Rainbow Coalition, as well as Ray Flynn's populist coalition, we have to appreciate the popular reaction that developed to the way Boston was governed from the early 1950s through the four-term Kevin White administration, 1968-1984. By 1983 both coalitions were fueled by real passion, grass-roots political enthusiasm, and class resentment. But if we are to understand the differences between the King and Flynn coalitions we must see how the policies of the White regime affected people of color in particular and we must review the long struggle over school desegregation. School busing was not a major issue in the 1983 election, despite King's efforts to make Flynn accountable for his anti-busing, pro-segregation record. But the core of each candidate's coalition took shape during the busing conflict that polarized the Hub in the mid-seventies, and in some subtle ways the 1983 campaign was fought along some of the same battle lines drawn during the desegregation conflict.

THE "NEW BOSTON" COALITION

Kevin White's four-term administration (1968-1984) was the longest and most successful of the liberal "pro-growth coalitions" that rose to power in many cities during the late 1960s.[10] Actually, the groundwork for White's regime was laid in the 1950s and early 1960s by a business/reform effort to create a New Boston out of a run-down, depressed city with machine-controlled government. During the last administration of Boston's colorful boss James Michael Curley (who left office for the last time in 1949) a business/reform coalition formed in response to an urban crisis caused by industrial decline, suburbanization, an eroding tax base, rising government expenses, and the "cancerous growth of the slums." All of these things made Boston an unattractive place for capitalist investors, as reflected in the remarkable absence of skyscrapers from Boston's skyline. The Brahmin business elite reacted with undisguised hostility to the city's arrogant, charismatic Mayor Curley. He showed little interest in downtown development, displayed blatant ethnic and class prejudice in awarding city jobs and setting tax rates, and brazenly escalated the cost of city government by expanding public employment. As the cost of city services rose and the tax base declined (due to industrial migration), Mayor Curley drastically boosted assessment rates on commercial and industrial property. Ephron Catlin, a senior official of the First National Bank in this period, recalls that in the minds of businessmen "there was a feeling that Boston was in the hands of the supercrooks. Nobody had ever seen an honest Irishman around here, in the Yankees' opinion. God, they hated Curley."[11]

After a fifty-year career in which he became kind of a folk hero to most working-class Bostonians, James Michael Curley lost in a close election to John Hynes, a bland young politician who had the backing of the New Boston Committee, a business-based reform group. As mayor, Hynes forged one of the country's first "pro-growth coalitions." It included a younger generation of ethnic politicians, "a new breed of government bureaucrats, large corporations, central business district real estate developers, merchant interests and the construction trades." The coalition also had the estimable support of Richard Cardinal Cushing, head of a very powerful Catholic archdiocese and an archrival of Mayor Curley, who failed in his last two attempts to regain City Hall in the 1950s.[12]

Using tax breaks, federal grants, and big-bank financing, the New Boston coalition pushed for highway construction, slum clearance, downtown development, and government efficiency. Hynes initiated the "clearance" of the New York Streets neighborhood where Mel King was born and raised, and then the infamous destruction of another multi-ethnic area, the West End, which displaced 2,600 families and warned inner-city residents what the New Boston had in store for them.[13] In 1959 a traditional machine politician from South Boston, John Powers, tried to revive the old Curley coalition and regain city hall from the ruling group. Powers caused the city's Brahmin bankers and bond holders to break into a cold sweat when he threatened that, if elected, he would declare bankruptcy to solve the city's fiscal crisis. Business leaders immediately formed a special coordinating group, soon dubbed "the Vault," and backed a pro-business candidate named John Collins who defeated Powers and began to reform city government, laying off 1,200 city workers and hiring New Haven's redevelopment czar Ed Logue to get on with "slum clearance."[14]

THE CIVIL RIGHTS MOVEMENT

During the 1960s Boston's highly segregated school and housing systems became targets of organizing and protest efforts that would lead to significant changes in city politics. In 1961 the NAACP sued the Boston Housing Authority for practicing de facto segregation and the courts found the BHA guilty. The public schools suffered both from the neglect of the city's new business leaders and the retrograde and blatantly racist practices of the old machine politicians who maintained control of the school committee and school department.[15] In 1960 Citizens for Boston Public Schools (CBPS) formed to protest conditions and a year later it ran four candidates for school committee. The two whites won and the two blacks lost. One of the losers was Mel King, a youth worker at United South End Settlements. In 1962 the Northern Student Movement, initiated to support civil rights struggles in the South, joined some black churches to set up tutorial programs. In 1962 the Citizens' group, the NAACP, and CORE all published reports critical of de facto segregation in Boston's schools and joined forces to pressure the school committee. When the committee refused to acknowledge de facto segregation, students boycotted the system. An unexpected 9,000 students (about one-quarter of the student body) participated in the Stay Out campaign of 1963 and many attended freedom schools modeled after those in the South. The civil rights movement in Boston kept the pressure up on all fronts. At the same time, Mel King led a STOP day and asked people to walk off their jobs to protest de facto segregation, police brutality, and other forms of discrimination. The NAACP and other established black leaders opposed the idea of a work stoppage and called their own demonstration, a memorial to slain civil rights leader Medgar Evers. But the two groups did come together in a "gesture of solidarity," marching through the South End while singing "Freedom, Freedom" and "We Shall Overcome"[16] to a rally on Boston Common.

In response, the school committee became more intransigent. The chairperson, Louise Day Hicks of South Boston, had been elected to "keep politics out of the schools" and at first appeared open-minded, but in 1963 she emerged as a leader of the white resistance to desegregation. That fall she campaigned for re-election on the race issue as a defender of segregation and the "neighborhood school." Indeed, during the summer of 1963 Hicks "identified herself as the budding symbol of northern intransigence toward civil rights demands," according to Peter Schrag. She also identified herself with Mayor Curley's populist legacy and claimed to represent the "little people" of South Boston and the city as a whole. She "resisted the whole establishment on behalf of small people who never expect to make it big." Hicks led all candidates in the 1963 election and Mel King failed to come close in his second bid for the school committee.[17]

During the mid-sixties Boston became a battleground of civil rights protest and white resistance around the issue of school segregation. The protest movement included parent boycotts, student strikes, dramatic school committee hearings, picket lines, marches, and the creation of "freedom schools," including one at South End Settlement House where Mel King was "principal." This agitation (highlighted by Martin Luther King's appearance on Boston Common) led to the passage of the state Racial Imbalance law in 1965, which demanded desegregation but prohibited busing as a solution. After a brief lull, boycotts continued, notably at the Gibson School described by Jonathan Kozol in *Death at an Early Age*. A new phase of the struggle began. Black demands for "community-controlled education" led both to voluntary plans for busing black children to suburbs and to the opening of private community schools in Roxbury. In 1965 Mel King and other citizens' candidates again confronted Louise Day Hicks for using the "fear-laden issue of busing and race for her own political advantage," but without success. Hicks won an impressive victory over the field because one in three citizens voted *only* for her. But Mel King came in sixth in the race for five seats, and for the first time in the city's history, a greater percentage of black voters than whites went to the polls in an off-year primary election. A direct line ran from the electoral mobilization created by civil rights struggles between 1961 and 1965 and the new level of black political activism in 1983.[18]

KEVIN H. WHITE'S REGIME AND INDEPENDENT BLACK POLITICS

In 1967 Louise Day Hicks decided to run for mayor on her segregationist record and her new reputation as a populist champion of the "little people" in poor white neighborhoods. This was also the year that Mel King became director of the New Urban League and began a program to help black parents confront school problems. And it was a year of intense black protest. Mothers for Adequate Welfare occupied the Roxbury welfare office at Grove Hall. When protestors gathered outside, the police rioted and looting and burning broke out afterwards on the black commercial strip. The police riot and Hicks's racist mayoralty campaign called for continued mobilization in the black community.

Kevin H. White, a new type of Irish politician from all-white West Roxbury, waged a liberal campaign against Hicks. He presented himself simultaneously as a reformer, as a developer who would continue plans for the New Boston, and Kennedy liberal who would restore racial peace. After an intense, bitter campaign, White beat Hicks by less than 5,000 votes. He won because he received over 15,000 black votes after a registration drive and a push to get out the vote led to an unprecedented 68 percent turnout among blacks. Along with Hicks's defeat, black and white supporters celebrated the election of Thomas Atkins, the first black elected to an at-large city council seat.

Once elected, Kevin White began to build a patronage machine modeled after Richard Daley's organization in Chicago with an important arm in the black community. White modernized the New Boston coalition by gaining more white liberal and black support. Though Kevin White governed more effectively than many of the liberal pro-business mayors of the era, he was not unopposed. First, the continuing mobilization of blacks and white allies against school desegregation took place independent of city hall and eventually led to the 1974 court-ordered busing plan which took the schools entirely out of the city government's hands. Second, there was less coherent but continuous unrest and protest over the pro-business development policies of the White administration which led to luxurious downtown growth while neighborhood business and housing suffered.

In 1968, White's first year in office, all of these opposition currents swirled through city politics. A third community-controlled black private school opened and the Black Panthers began a free breakfast program and visits to white teachers' classrooms. Parents and students continued to boycott the schools at certain times. In one incident a student was suspended from English High for wearing a dashiki, and black students walked out in protest, joined by some whites. The Black Student Union was organized. And in 1968 the first black labor union in modern times was formed. The United Community Construction Workers (UCCW) aimed to fight against discrimination by contractors and unions. The assassination of Martin Luther King led to violent protest, and in its aftermath activists created a Black United Front (BUF) which included many important groups (though not the NAACP, which was apparently offended by the group's nationalist politics). When confronted by the Front's demand for community-controlled development funds, Mayor White listened but then tried to co-opt the BUF by forming his own group, the Boston Urban Foundation, with the same initials. At the same time housing struggles intensified. The South End, a battleground during this stage of urban renewal, produced a strong neighborhood advocacy group, CAUSE, and two tenant unions, one of them a Hispanic organization. In 1968 CAUSE members, including Mel King, occupied a Redevelopment Authority office in the South End to protest inadequate relocation plans. Then they picketed a parking lot in the South End where the Redevelopment Authority had bulldozed liveable buildings, displacing one hundred families. When CAUSE members blocked the parking lot, twenty-three were arrested, including Mel King. Tent City was then erected on the site which has since become a symbol of popular resistance to the city's pro-business housing policies.[19]

Black people supported Kevin White in his 1967 contest against Louise Day Hicks because they hoped he would change some of these policies. They have been disappointed. The sixteenth anniversary of Tent City is this year and the site is still vacant. Apparently a new luxury shopping center will use the land for parking and there will be no new affordable housing. The support the black community generated for Kevin White in 1967 was not qualified or unequivocal. Though White attempted to bring some black loyalists into his organization, he could not subdue the strong streak of independence that had been evident in Boston black politics for a long time.

As early as 1926 black political leaders split with the Republican Party and tried to seek leverage with their small but often crucial vote in close nonpartisan preliminary elections. In 1935 a united front formed, including Democrats, Republicans, Socialists, and Communists, to nominate black candidates for city office. Though lack of a strong political machine has suggested weakness, in fact, as James Jennings argues, the independence of the black vote meant that democratic politicians, including Curley, often courted it assiduously. A small patronage organization attached to the Democratic Party did emerge during the 1950s when the black population increased significantly.[20] And in 1958 the leaders of the organization helped one of their members win election to the State House. But this black "machine," which taught Mel King his first lessons in electoral politics, had very limited patronage. It fit into the "service stage" of political development which, according to King, involved "taking the white power structure's handouts rather than organizing the community to demand satisfaction of black needs."[21]

Of course Mayor White tried to prolong the "service stage" in black community development, but as events in the late sixties showed, a new "organizing stage" had already begun quite independent of the Democratic Party.[22] For instance, in 1971 two-term City Councilor Thomas Atkins decided to challenge Mayor White in the preliminary, even though the contest also included Louise Day Hicks and even though the mayor aggressively wooed black voters. White again faced Hicks in the final. After pushing very hard for black and Latino registration, he won the election by a big margin. But this time White's victory over Hicks did not depend on his black vote. And so the mayor began to build a stronger base in white working-class areas that had been solidly for Hicks, and where he was known as "Mayor Black" because of his promises to voters in Roxbury. White could now pay less attention to the Afro-American community because he thought he could always count on black votes if he faced a more conservative white candidate in the final. It also meant that city hall would be less helpful with voter registration.[23]

White incorrectly assumed, however, that he could take the black vote for granted. If anything black voters were becoming more independent. In 1971, along with the Atkins challenge to the mayor, a militant black woman named Patricia Bonner-Lyons ran for school committee. Even though she attacked White and made no secret of her Communist Party affiliation, she gained a solid black vote and nearly won. In 1972 Mel King, by now a well-recognized militant and critic of city hall, won election to the State House from a mixed district with a white plurality.

THE BUSING CRISIS

In 1972 a group of black parents, supported by the NAACP, brought suit against the school committee in federal district court to challenge the continuing and increasing school segregation. Judge Arthur W. Garrity issued his decision on June 21, 1974 and ordered the school committee to implement his busing plan that September. Massive and violent white opposition surfaced, led by School Committee chairman John Kerrigan and City Councilor Louise Day Hicks. There were doubts about the court order in the black community, not only regarding the safety of children, but also over the lack of community control involved in the plan. State Rep. Mel King had tried to develop an alternative plan that allowed blacks more control of schools in their neighborhoods and would eventually make a majority of teachers in those areas black, but the Boston Teachers Union killed the plan, refusing to give up control over any jobs.[24]

When school busing began in September of 1974 and white crowds attacked black students and other people of color, the black community and its white allies rallied to defend students' rights to a safe, desegregated education. As the violence continued through the fall of 1974 and it became apparent that the White administration and the police department would not take sufficient steps to protect black people, Mel King and others wondered if they "were doing the right thing" by supporting busing. Mel had his answer when he talked to a black student being bused to South Boston High School. "We have to go," she declared with passion. "If they run us out of that school they can run us out of the city." For this student, and for many other people of color, busing was not "just a matter of education; it was an intensely political experience" from which hundreds of young black people got a very practical education. They would come to play a big role in Mel King's campaigns for mayor.[25]

While black leaders and parents rallied at Freedom House in

Roxbury to try to "keep calm in the black community and to prepare ... children for the harsh realities that awaited them in formerly all-white schools," something very different happened in white areas.[26] Political leaders like Hicks and local organizers mobilized through organizations like ROAR (Restore Our Alienated Rights) and stirred up white resistance in a threatening situation already filled with racial hatred. Ray Flynn, then a state representative for South Boston, strongly supported ROAR, marched in its demonstrations, and emerged as "one of the leaders of the anti-busing movement." During the 1983 campaign Flynn claimed to have been a moderating force within South Boston, but his public stance was anything but moderate, especially his bill to abolish compulsory schooling and his votes against the Racial Imbalance Act.[27]

Race had been the key issue in Boston politics ever since 1963 when Louise Day Hicks ran for school committee as a defender of segregated education. During the 1974 busing crisis groups like ROAR pushed politicians like Ray Flynn to be more outspoken defenders of de facto segregation and more obstructive opponents of busing. Just the opposite happened in black politics. In 1974 a new State Senate seat was created in a primarily black district. An established leader, State Rep. Royal Bolling, Sr., faced Bill Owens, a younger, more militant state representative. Owens had been directly involved in the movement against segregation as one of the parents who organized one of the first community schools in Roxbury. He campaigned as a supporter of mandatory busing and as an outspoken critic of racist politicians in Boston. Owens defeated Bolling in a divisive contest, making an issue of Bolling's support for a voluntary busing plan to replace the court-ordered plan. During the fall of 1974 Senator-elect Owens provided leadership for a large militant march against racism and in favor of busing. Up to this time few socialists, except those in the Communist Party, had been involved directly in anti-racist work.[28] Now many younger left activists became deeply involved in supporting the black struggle for desegregation. This anti-racist work laid the basis for their involvement in the 1983 campaign.

While white politicians moved to the right and some black politicians moved to the left, the White administration antagonized both camps with its inconsistent policies and obvious desire to save face during the crisis.

THE GROWING CRISIS OF THE WHITE ADMINISTRATION

While White tried, not too successfully, to avoid responsibility for the busing conflict, his housing and development policies continued to generate grass-roots opposition, and the mayor could not escape responsibility for those policies. Indeed, during White's first three terms, Boston became a prime example of a city in which neighborhood residents mobilized against pro-business development policies. As neighborhood opposition to new Boston priorities continued, city hall turned away from slum clearance policies and the blatant land grabbing of the Redevelopment Authority and focused more on fancy downtown projects like the suburban/tourist oriented Quincy Market.[29] For example, in the South End, busing was not a problem, but poor and working-class residents and their professional allies organized against the luxury housing developers who were given a free hand and lucrative tax breaks by city hall to "rehabilitate" the area's beautiful brick bow-front houses, thus displacing the poor and elderly from the multi-national, low-rent district. By 1974, when some of the white gentry in the South End brought suit to stop the development of public, low-income housing, even the mayor bemoaned the growing inner-city class struggle over housing between the "haves" and "have nots." What he did not say was that his own housing policies were to blame.[30]

White managed to keep a governing coalition together despite major community protests against his policies, an inner-city class struggle over housing, and the extreme racial conflict over busing. He proved far more adept than most of his contemporaries at responding to crises that threatened to rip apart his pro-business coalition. While other liberals gave way to "cop mayors" like Rizzo in Philadelphia or to black mayors like Young in Detroit, Kevin White stayed the course and continued to build up a patronage machine second only to the Daley organization in Chicago.[31]

In 1975 White won reelection to a third term over Joseph Timilty, a more conservative white politician who had alienated most blacks. But support for White was soft as turnout fell in the black wards and discontent with racial violence and jobs turned to resentment. Moreover, the State House Black Caucus was divided. According to Mel King, a caucus member at the time, conflicts emerged between those "building personal power and those dedicated to empowering the community," especially in efforts to "fight police harassment, a serious problem in Boston." "Some black elected officials thought that the demands being made by the community would be too radical," King writes in his book *Chain of Change*. Some also felt that meeting these demands would jeopardize their standing with the black middle class. "But how could any Black official be 'too radical,'" King asked, "given the oppression confronting the great majority of Black people in Boston?"[32] Mel King has been answering this question with principled action for many years. His consistency and courage continued to gain him credibility among black leaders even though he was still unable to bring them together in an "independent political organization." As conditions worsened in the seventies Mel King maintained his radicalism as a personal conviction; but it also *reflected* more than ever the oppression of Boston's hard-pressed black community.

PROGRESSIVE BLACK POLITICS

Though progressive black politicians like King and Owens had success in the early seventies, division still existed not only on the question of militancy but on the question of loyalty to the White organization. The mayor not only used patronage as a carrot; he used his office to undermine independent politics in the black community. He employed patronage to reward friends and to punish enemies and to nurture cooperative black political leadership. He also created an impressive public relations operation to preserve his image as a liberal and he manipulated various electoral processes, including voter registration, to his advantage. Though White encouraged minority voter registration to defeat Hicks in 1967 and used city hall to do so when he faced her again in 1971, his Election Department became less helpful in the seventies. In fact, the number of registered black voters actually dropped in the three predominantly black wards from 28,637 at the start of White's administration to 20,069 in 1979. This resulted in part from lack of support for registration, from growing opposition to White, and from continuing frustration with the at-large system of city elections which made it very difficult for minority candidates to gain elected office.[33]

In 1977 a plan emerged to return to district representation, which Yankee reformers had replaced with at-large elections in a futile attempt to limit Irish political power. Mel King, who helped initiate the plan, rallied black support. Politicians from areas like South Boston who had been successful in at-large elections vehemently opposed the plan and Mayor White did not support it. It lost by only a few thousand votes.[34]

Black support for district representation was not diminished by the fact that a black person did win election to the school committee at-large for the first time since the early 1900s, when there was still district representation. John O'Bryant, who gained this important victory in 1977, had been a guidance counselor and teacher for fifteen years and had struggled against the system from within.[35] O'Bryant was a close ally and friend of Mel King and had managed two of Mel's unsuccessful campaigns for the school committee in the sixties. O'Bryant was independent of the White administration and he showed that a progressive black candidate could be successful in a citywide race. He was also a skilled political organizer who knew the importance of mobilizing the black community independently. In 1978 O'Bryant led a group that included Mel King in forming the progressive Black Political Task Force, which called for the empowerment of people of color and made other demands, including full employment and "the redistribution of goods and services."[36] What James Jennings, a member of the task force, calls the "new face" of progressive black politics was clearly visible in Boston by 1978.[37]

In 1979 Mel King decided to challenge Kevin White in the preliminary election. The effort represented a "process" and a move away from the politics of personality toward decentralization and participation. He renewed the struggle for district representation and began pulling together a coalition of the various new social movements against discrimination and repression, with the intention of building a "structure" that would endure after the election. During the summer a network of white leftists and Third World militants active in anti-racist work staged an impressive concert called "Amandla: A Festival of Unity" featuring Bob Marley. Mel King appeared with Marley before a crowd of 15,000 and connected the problems of racism in Boston with those in southern Africa whose liberation groups would benefit from the concert's proceeds. Many of those leftists who produced Amandla would also be involved in Mel's campaign.

Although Kevin White maintained the loyalty of some black voters and some leaders, notably the ministers, King won a majority of the black vote in 1979 and finished a surprising third in the preliminary with a total of 15 percent. Though he maintained his militancy and raised little money, King had demonstrated the promise of progressive black politics.[38]

After the election King's supporters formed the Boston People's Organization.[39] The BPO might have provided a basis for more unity between black and white progressives if it had not been stymied by long debates over process and program which discouraged participation by ordinary working-class people. The BPO tried to be everything to everybody rather than to focus narrowly on local neighborhood issues or to become primarily an electoral organization to carry on with the kind of agenda Mel King campaigned on in 1979. The organization failed to hold black participation after the election, partly due to the insistence of some organized white leftists on playing leadership roles. The BPO took part in the unsuccessful effort to defeat the tax-cutting referendum Proposition 2½ in 1980 and played a key role in the effective 1982 campaign for charter reform and district representation. This victory injected real energy into political efforts by feminists, gays, lesbians, and people of color who could now concentrate their power in a few district elections instead of being all disenfranchised by the at-large system. This important democratic reform also laid the groundwork for Mel King's 1983 campaign and for the district campaigns of several left candidates including Charles Yancey, a black progressive, and David Scondras, a gay activist, tenant organizer, and member of Democratic Socialists of America; both were elected to the city council. Several of the leading white BPO activists took important positions in Mel King's campaign, but the organization itself did not survive. Indeed, the Rainbow Coalition superseded it and hoped to succeed where its predecessor failed.

Progressive black politics gained momentum rapidly after 1978 for various reasons: a) the success of black candidates for school committee (O'Bryant won re-election in 1979 and was elected Chair in 1981, when a black woman, Jean McGuire, joined him on the committee); b) the impact of Mel King's surprising third place showing in the 1979 mayoral elections; and c) the emergence of a new generation of young black political activists who came of age during what Mel called the "organizing stage" of community development and had taken part in the difficult struggles for desegregation.

Moreover, mass discontent began to surface with the destructive policies and broken promises of the White administration. Boston had become a more dangerous city than ever before for people of color. Even after the stonings of school buses subsided, other racist attacks continued. Black homes were attacked in white areas. Twelve black women were murdered in six months during 1979 provoking angry protest over official lack of concern. A black high school football player was shot down on a field in white Charlestown and permanently paralyzed. And the police shot and killed three black men without being brought to justice. All of these outrages led to anti-racist organizing and defense work; and at the same time they certainly convinced many people of color that the White administration would not protect them.

Mel King's 1979 campaign also helped to raise longterm economic and social grievances. Indeed, during White's regime employment conditions for people of color actually worsened in the private sector. A recent EEOC study showed that blacks lost ground in scores of industries during the last several years. Minorities were underrepresented in many clerical and sales jobs that required minimum training and few specialized skills, even though minority people in Boston are better educated than their counterparts in other cities.[40] Mayor White could hardly defend the unimpressive level of minority hiring in city jobs that took place during his tenure, and of course he could take no credit for minority hiring that resulted from court suits against the police, fire, and school departments which had remained lily white during his first two terms. He also stood aside during the bitter struggle of the United Community Construction Workers to apply "the Philadelphia Plan" for minority affirmative action hiring in the construction industry, a fight which ended up in the courts and not in city hall.[41]

Faced with a recession and unemployment in 1973, the UCCW had turned toward a new strategy of allying with other minority workers. In 1975 the once all-black union reached out to Hispanic and Asian workers. Blacks gave up some of their power in order to make the union more democratic and representative, an important point in the making of the Rainbow Coalition. They then secured federal money to set up the Third World Jobs Clearing House. And in 1977, under Mel King's leadership, minority workers developed a Boston Jobs for Boston Residents program that also reached out to white workers who lived in the city. The Boston Jobs program demanded that a minimum of 50 percent of the total workforce, craft by craft, be composed of Boston residents on all publicly funded or subsidized development projects in the city. A minimum of 25 percent had to be minority workers and a minimum of 10 percent women. When negotiations over the policy broke down, King began to push Mayor White on the issue during the 1979 campaign, and the mayor responded by trying to co-opt King's support: first with an executive order on minority hiring, and then by making the quotas in the King jobs campaign binding.[42] (Once reelected, White let the matter ride until the Supreme Court declared the Boston jobs residency program constitutional in 1983.)

Though White's public relations people tried to give him the credit for his policy, black workers knew that Mel King was responsible. King's hope that the Boston Jobs Coalition, formed in 1978, would attract white workers who lived in the city remained unfulfilled, however. The white construction unions, whose members lived largely outside the city, opposed the residency program tooth and nail. But the quotas the jobs coalitions advocated did affect hiring on the big Southwest Corridor project and the massive Copley Place enterprise, where newly elected Mayor Ray Flynn has promised to make sure the King hiring quotas are enforced. Now that the residency policy is an ordinance construction unions may try to evade it, but the fact remains that far more minority workers and women will now be employed in construction and in service jobs—and they can be unionized if they can be convinced that the unions are not their enemies.

Under the White administration business boomed and jobs were created, but more for suburbanites than citydwellers. The city added 50,000 new jobs after 1970 but by the end of that decade 65 percent of the new jobs belonged to commuters.[43] A key test for the future will be whether more white workers will see their interests as tied to the development of progressive black politics and the Rainbow Coalition, rather than to the conservative politics of the white trade unions and old-fashioned pols. King, though he seems anti-union in some of his statements, has reached out to white workers in both of his citywide campaigns, asking them to side with the interest of the 80 percent who remain unorganized and unrecognized by unions instead of the 20 percent who are mobilized by union leaders interested *only* in preserving limited privileges.

THE HOUSING ISSUE AND FAIR SHARE POPULISM

Housing became a terrible problem for poor and blue-collar working people during White's tenure as mayor. Development projects like Copley Place created new jobs and tax revenues, but they drove up the cost of housing in nearby areas like the South End and accelerated the pace of gentrification. During the early seventies I lived in a South End lodging house, the kind of dwelling that once provided shelter for thousands of single and retired workers who paid only a few dollars a week for a furnished room. In 1965 nearly a thousand lodging houses still existed in the South End, but by 1974, after luxury condo and apartment developers sunk their fangs into the property, only 250 remained. Now there are just 37. As a result of White's development policies many lodgers have been forced to live with their families or have ended up in the streets.[44] White's housing policies also removed 18,000 rental units from the market during the seventies. About half were demolished and the other half rehabilitated as high-cost housing.

While the cost of housing and other necessities soared, the incomes of working-class Bostonians failed to rise significantly. In 1980 the Hub was rated as having one of the lowest median family incomes of any major city ($16,062) and one of the highest cost of living figures. Under White's administration the downtown prospered and became "the most integrated financial service center in the U.S. outside of New York" with $300 billion of capital in its bank vaults. Inner-city neighborhoods were gentrified, eight new luxury hotels were started or completed, and fashionable stores and boutiques popped up with dazzling frequency. The contrast between the haves and have nots became glaring.[45]

The city did nothing to ease the housing shortage for the working class. In fact conditions worsened. A few militant groups won victories, like the Hispanic tenant union, Inquilinos Boricuas en Accion, which developed its own community-controlled housing in the South End. But existing public housing suffered from criminal neglect as thousands of units were removed from public use. The situation was so bad that the courts put the Boston Housing Authority into a receivership. According to court-appointed administrator Harry Spence, "There has been a sense at some level in city hall over the last fifteen years that there are just too many poor people in this city and too much subsidized housing, and that if they just let public housing slide, [the poor] will go away. Besides being a peculiarly malicious policy, it won't work—poor people can't go away."[46]

Mel King's activism on the housing issue was well known, at least among black and Hispanic people and white people in the South End and the other neighborhoods he represented in the State House. His leadership became obvious in 1968 when he was arrested at the Tent City site. His activism brought him into direct conflict with the White administration. As Mel wrote of South End housing policies, "While racism and lack of government protection pushed people of color out of white working-class areas, government planning [continued to push] people of color out of the South End to make way for the 'gentry.'"[47]

While King championed the cause of those most oppressed by the housing situation—that is, people of color—Ray Flynn, also a state rep during the seventies, took a more general approach to the housing crisis. He became a strong advocate of public housing, rent control, and strict rules on condominium conversion. These policies also brought him into conflict with the White government and allowed him to take advantage of the organizing led by citizen-action movements, whose leaders adopted a populist approach that ignored racism as a central issue in housing struggles.

White working-class people, especially the elderly, had serious problems with the housing situation whether they were over-taxed home-owners, evicted lodging-house dwellers, tenants, or owners who worried about blockbusting. Initially the disaffection with White's housing and development policies came from black or mixed areas like the South End.[48] And at first white working-class areas did not mobilize against urban renewal, assuming they could not fight city hall.

During the early seventies student radicals moved into white working-class areas like East Boston and Dorchester to start organizing projects, community newspapers, and, in Dorchester, a Tenant Action Committee. Some of these people had been involved in Harvard-Radcliffe SDS and the Indochina Peace Campaign. Others were sponsored by liberal churches. Two of these radicals, Michael Ansara and Ira Arlook, decided to organize white working-class youth alienated by the war and the economy. They started The People First (TPF) in Dorchester and focused on removing a corrupt, tyrannical judge who employed blatantly racist sentencing policies. TPF did attract some angry young white people, connected with the Vietnam Vets Against the War and got rid of the obnoxious judge (on corruption charges). But it soon fell apart as ex-student radicals dropped in and out of the project and conflicts erupted between the indigenous youth and the outside left leaders.[49] Then Ansara found liberal grant money to open the Boston Community School in 1973. It provided resources and courses for community activists and newspapers like the *Dorchester Community News*. The school also housed the CAP Energy program, an effort concerned with utilities, and Nine to Five, founded by Karen Nussbaum, a member of the Harvard group, and dedicated to organizing women office workers.

At the same time a few other student radicals, some of them from the Northern Student Movement, had come to work with the Dorchester Tenant Action Committee. In 1973 DTAC changed from being a tenant organization to a broader group that included homeowners. The new Dorchester Community Action Council (DCAC) still fought for rent control but also took up issues like neighborhood deterioration that affected both tenants and homeowners. Though homeowners could not be expected to support rent control, they were the "key actors" in deciding what should be done about issues like blockbusting, redlining, and abandoned housing. DCAC worked in integrated neighborhoods and constantly encountered whites who believed that neighborhoods deteriorated *because* blacks moved in. So organizers tried to zero in on the institutionalized racism of bankers and real estate interests who busted up white neighborhoods and then victimized blacks who followed. Instead of taking what one DCAC organizer called the "liberal approach" of saying to whites that blacks were just the same as they were, they focused on the common enemy of both groups. Personal racism was handled privately, and occasional racist attacks were publicly condemned, but the focus remained on the destructive, divisive policies of banks and real estate companies.

In 1976 DCAC merged with CAP Energy and a new group called Fair Share working in Chelsea, Waltham, and East Boston. The new organization, Mass. Fair Share, headed by Michael Ansara of the Community School, built up a large statewide membership by hiring students on a commission basis to canvass door to door. The organization received good publicity for its local campaigns on street repairs, playgrounds, schools, housing, taxes, and utilities. It also carried on the work of DCAC in racially troubled Dorchester, where it was difficult to find a neutral site to have an inter-racial meeting.[50] In this tense setting Fair Share did organize a number of block clubs in a black and Hispanic area, and in the aftermath of busing it did begin to "forge alliances between blacks and working-class whites on issues that transcended race."[51]

Fair Share's appeal to people of color was limited, however, by its organizers' approach to racism. Like the early *Dorchester Community News* and DCAC, the organization refused to take a stand for desegregation through busing, or to make racism itself an issue. As late as 1980 some of the staff expressed distress when the Fair Share convention voted to endorse the Catholic Church's anti-racist Covenant of Justice, Equity and Harmony.[52] Charlotte Ryan, a community organizer who worked on the *Dorchester Community News*, observed that while many individual organizers in Fair Share were personally concerned with fighting racism, they did so in a private way. Unlike Louise Day Hicks and Ray Flynn, the anti-busing populist politicians, these organizers would "never use racism to build a popular base" and indeed sought to defuse it by emphasizing "winnable, nondivisive issues" that "transcended" race. But by taking a strictly economic approach to problems that would yield "quick victories," "they ignored and sometimes denied the racial component of issues," according to Ryan, who shared this view of organizing when she began her work in Dorchester. As a person of Irish working-class origins and a member of a trade union family, she took the populist view that you could "unite people around common economic grievances without addressing racism directly." She opposed busing as a divisive plan. However, after working in the black and Latino sections of Dorchester, Charlotte Ryan came to feel that she had a "white person's view of racism." "It wasn't something I lived with everyday as black people did. Like other white people I didn't see how the world was divided on race and I didn't have the door slammed in my face all the time just because of my race. People of color couldn't choose whether or not to make racism an issue, like the white organizers did. If you were black in Boston you couldn't escape the issue."

RAY FLYNN'S POPULIST COALITION

Given their populist view of racism it was logical for Fair Share organizers to support Ray Flynn's campaign for mayor in 1983.

Though Flynn had not come to his populism via the anti-war movement and community organizing, he did adopt an economistic approach to the issues, especially housing, that basically resembled Fair Share's approach.

Flynn's campaign staff, which included several progressives on the populist left, knew that he would maintain his conservative, anti-busing constituency no matter what, so they wanted to emphasize his changed position on issues like the Equal Rights Amendment and anti-discrimination housing laws which he at one time opposed. Flynn had worked closely with the Massachusetts Tenants Organization (MTO) formed in 1981, and used his position on the city council to become a leading supporter of rent control and banning condominium conversion. The MTO leadership endorsed Flynn over King because, according to one leader, he was more "visible" on the housing issue, though King's voting record was every bit as good. Though Fair Share did not endorse anyone formally, its leaders and many members worked for Flynn, who benefitted from the single-issue organizing efforts these groups made in white areas. Support from liberal leaders in MTO, Nine to Five, and the Elder Americans also helped Flynn's effort to present himself as a progressive—in spite of his very conservative voting record on social issues, including prominent leadership of a sustained fight against publicly funded abortions.

Though Flynn did attract some white liberal support, his coalition consisted principally of white working-class people hurt by the policies of the new Boston which favored the downtown over their neighborhoods. This anger became more palpable when White began closing schools and fire and police stations in white areas in an effort to pressure the legislature to approve emergency fiscal aid for the city in the wake of the tax-cutting Proposition 2½. Ironically, the effects of the measure angered even the taxpayers who voted for it and then saw their services cut back, and their jobs threatened by public employee cutbacks. Under these circumstances, unionized public employees who had lived with or by the patronage system became surprisingly agitated with the city's unfair policies of hiring, firing, and promotion. This was especially true in the police, fire, and teachers unions, which had become alienated from White and strongly supported Flynn. Of course much of that alienation was also directed against black public employees hired and retained as a result of affirmative action court cases. Flynn made no effort to correct the impression that he opposed affirmative action. Finally, though neither candidate wished to arouse the bitter feelings connected with busing, Flynn maintained his adamant opposition to the court order and naturally captured the conservative white voters.

Though Flynn and his progressive supporters claimed to want minority support for a governing coalition that would "bring the city together," a straight economic appeal lacked credibility to people of color. Flynn's strained argument that the issues were the same in South Boston and Roxbury contrasted strongly with Mel King's insistence on making an issue of the "incredibly high level of racism" in Boston. Flynn even objected to using the term racism and denied the city's bigoted past. "The real problem is economic discrimination," he said in an important TV debate. "There are poor whites and blacks who do not have access to the political power structure in this city" and whose neighborhoods shared none of the downtown's economic wealth.[53] Flynn's staff shared this populist-economist approach to the issues and believed that it would be divisive to confront racism and make it an issue. Flynn's campaign manager, a former student radical, Ray Dooley, told me that Mel King's insistence on making racism an issue actually damaged the city's prospects for racial peace and made King appear as the "black candidate." Dooley seemed to think that racism was a leftist issue, not the central issue for people of color or the key problem in working-class life generally. The social democrats in Flynn's campaign were very sensitive to criticisms from the left, but they were far more worried about being branded as leftists themselves and therefore embraced pragmatic reform politics.

The Flynn campaign's appeal for economic unity and fear of divisive issues like racism harkened back to earlier populist and reform movements which emphasized good government and economic justice as the best antidotes to discrimination. These movements advocated economic democracy (now the slogan of the new populist and social democratic left), but not social equality which implied race-mixing and integration. It was much easier to attack Wall Street and assume that all oppressed people would be united by common economic grievances than it was to take up the difficult struggle for equal rights. Ray Flynn's socialist and progressive advisors repeated some past mistakes by assuming that racism and other forms of discrimination could be avoided as political issues and that economic reforms alone could bring people together. Such false idealism has never had much appeal to groups like women and blacks whose oppression cannot be lifted just through economic reform.[54]

The original Southern populists attacked the worst effects of racism, like lynching, but they did not address racial bigotry in their own ranks. Instead, they counted on common economic grievances to unite black and white farmers; but because of racism and the legacy of slavery, the lot of white yeomen and tenants differed significantly from that of black sharecroppers. Indeed, blacks had to respond cautiously to the populist appeal for economic unity because for them "there was no purely 'economic' way out." White populists did not confront racial differences and conflicts within their coalition and tried to "dissociate themselves from the 'race problem.'" Therefore racism could be used more easily to destroy the movement and it could reappear much more quickly within the ranks of defeated white populists, as the tragic career of Tom Watson suggests. As leader of the Georgia People's Party, Watson made an heroic attempt to unite black and white farmers in the 1890s, but when the Party was defeated, he turned to racist demogoguery and became a leading spokesman for anti-Semitism, anti-Catholicism and anti-radicalism. The classic problem for populism a century ago remains a problem today. Populists promise equal opportunity and "fair shares" through democratic reform and economic justice, but they usually fail to attack the structure of social inequality or to combat the discriminatory attitudes that can easily poison inter-racial coalitions.[55]

Ray Flynn adopted a populist "fair shares" approach to equality, rather than the "equal shares" approach advocated by Mel King.[56] Flynn apparently believes that if the voters elect a "man of the people" who identifies with the neighborhoods as against downtown interests and that if he refrains from creating an "unfair" patronage system, then everyone has a good chance of getting their "fair share" of housing, services, and jobs in spite of the way the private housing and job markets work and in spite of the blatant favoritism that has always controlled the distribution of employment and services in Boston. The implication: there is no need for binding affirmative action and militant struggle on the part of women, people of color, gays, and lesbians. Indeed, during the campaign Flynn gave no hint that he understood the structural bases of racism and sexism or the cultural and psychological bases of prejudice that make discrimination a problem even with full employment and adequate housing. He seemed to feel that his personal stand against discrimination, combined with strong law enforcement, would satisfy oppressed groups. He did speak movingly about the "hidden injuries of class" including his own family's experience of being on welfare.[57] And like many Boston Irish, he has a strong sense of anti-Catholic oppression. But Flynn generalized too easily from his own experience without trying to understand the special circumstances of women, people of color, gays, and lesbians. For example, when the two candidates appeared before women's groups, Flynn was asked how he would respond to violent attacks against women and gay men. His answer was to hire more police! Mel retorted that the police were part of the problem. When asked to define sexism Flynn seemed at a loss for words. King responded to questions from a feminist perspective.

Despite all the rhetoric about bringing the city back together, Flynn ran a very conventional, cautious campaign, designed to maintain the conservative white support he had marshalled as a South Boston politician. There was a strong restorationist tone to his populism, an appeal to return to the days when Curley was mayor and "the little people" were well-represented, a desire to go back to the neighborhoods when there was no crime and no struggle over housing, to preserve the Church's traditional teaching on the family and abortion, and even the neighborhood school as it existed before busing. He emphasized restoring services and jobs to the working-class people left out of Kevin White's development plans and patronage networks. It is not clear, though, how Flynn will do this without creating his own patronage regime, just as Curley and White did, and using it to reward friends and punish enemies. If he succumbs to politics as usual, which is what many of his hard-core supporters want, he will never be able to create the broad-based governing coalition he promised to build after the election.[58]

MEL KING'S RAINBOW COALITION

The Rainbow Coalition that formed around Mel King's candidacy also included people hurt by the New Boston and it too responded to the struggle of the neighborhoods against downtown interests. Its constituents felt even more excluded from Kevin White's patronage organization than did the members of Flynn's coalition. The King movement, however, emerged directly from the struggle for school desegregation and Flynn's came from the fight against it. This difference in origin accounts in part for other significant political differences. Take left support for example. Flynn won the support of the populist left concerned mainly with "non-divisive" economic issues, and King won the support of the women's movement, the anti-racist movement, the gay and lesbian movements, and the anti-imperialist and peace movements, as well as independent socialists who saw clear connections between issues of poverty, racism, sexism, imperialism, and the arms race. To take this a bit further one rarely saw Fair Share as an organization, or significant elements of the populist left, at the various Boston rallies and demonstrations concerning issues like nuclear arms, divestment in South Africa, U.S. intervention in Central America, or on behalf of safe streets for women, reproductive rights, gay pride, or Puerto Rican nationalism. And Ray Flynn's presence would have been unimaginable. Mel King was almost always there, linking the issues on what he called the "chain of change" and taking what he humorously called "a whole left approach." This gave the Rainbow Coalition much more than a feeling of outgroups getting together to put their chosen leader in city hall. It felt like a movement, but this time it was a multi-issue, multi-group movement that really seemed integrated.

Ray Flynn appealed to a desire to restore the past status of the neighborhoods in the romanticized age of James Michael Curley. Mel King made a broader appeal to community based on a solidarity of struggle in Boston that transcended neighborhood lines. And King's strong ties to the Latin and Asian communities allowed him to reach out to unify different communities of color and to include groups like lesbians, gays, and feminists, groups whose identities and agendas were not neighborhood-based for the most part. For these groups there was little to restore or romanticize about the political past in Boston. So Mel King helped give the Rainbow Coalition a vision of a future based on a unification of the new social movements. This sense of cultural unity and an almost utopian vision of the future contrasted strongly with Flynn's conventional campaign and attracted thousands of people alienated from electoral politics entirely.

Mel King's genuine sense of democracy, his universal ideas of community as well as his respect for the dignity and autonomy of various social groups and movements, let a hundred flowers bloom during the preliminary campaign. But during the final King seemed to abdicate leadership in certain areas to campaign strategists who wanted to centralize the effort and organize it along neighborhood lines. Various radical activists in the campaign have explained how this hurt efforts to organize autonomous constituency groups like blacks, gays, and lesbians.

King himself gave mixed messages. Clearly his whole political career personified black cultural pride and political independence, but Mel King has never been a separatist. Throughout the campaign he reached out to white citizens and appealed to their best instincts. He often reminded leftists and militants in his campaign to treat people in white areas as potential allies, as "people the same as you and me." He showed by his words and actions that he respected white people more than their own political leaders did. For example, he expressed outrage at the way demagogues constantly reminded the Boston Irish of their oppression, but instead of creating something positive out of their people's anger, they used it to create a "hostile defensive mentality."[59] He actively sought white supporters, not by assuring them that people of color had exactly the same problems, or by ignoring the divisive issues of racism and bigotry. He used his Boston Jobs residency program to appeal for unity between white and minority workers in the city but he also attacked the white unions for refusing to support affirmative action. Unlike Ray Flynn, who ignored a historic opportunity to address his white supporters on the subject of racism, King insisted that people who practiced or condoned discrimination were also hurt by it. He appealed not only to people's economic self-interest, but to their self-respect as human beings.

During the preliminary campaign, King visited the largely Irish section of Savin Hill in Dorchester where a black man had been killed by a subway train while trying to escape a gang of white youths. King asked to address a white citizens' meeting on the causes and consequences of this incident. "Look," he said, "the other candidates won't come here and talk to you about the problem of race. And that's because they don't respect you enough to think you can deal with the issue. But here we have a situation of a black man dead, and his family grieving. We have young white people in jail accused of murder and their families are in agony. White and black people are at odds in this city, but tell me, who won this one?"

How do you evaluate the effects of such a campaign? It was clearly the first time most white people in the city were addressed so clearly and so eloquently on the issue of racism. Perhaps the ground was not prepared in the white areas so that King could appeal to voters there on a range of issues. Perhaps making racism the issue in his campaign cost him votes. I doubt it. In any case this was an important step in the anti-racist struggle in Boston, and clearly exposed the opportunism of Ray Flynn's populist notion that racism need not be confronted head on because it was largely a matter of economic competition. There will never be an easy, inviting opportunity to confront white people about racism. Mel King made the most of his opportunity even in areas where the groundwork had not been laid.

Few movements in U.S. history have actually involved white people learning from black people's struggles. The Rainbow Coalition in Boston actually began this way. It was based on a historic mobilization of black people that began in the early 1960s with the fight against de facto segregation and Mel King's first city wide campaigns for school committee. In 1983 the mobilization included the Asian and Hispanic communities and various social movements composed of white people, largely but not entirely progressive in orientation. Perhaps the lesson they learned was largely lost on the vast white majority who elected Ray Flynn mayor. In any case, that majority should look at the city's black history again and think twice about the future. In the past decade the black population increased significantly, the other Third World population leapt up by 100 percent, and the white population declined. If present trends continue, by 1990 people of color in Boston will be the majority. As Mel King says, other movements have much to learn from the black struggle, which has "gone through all the stages of developing consciousness and competence and has come to the point where they are prepared to enter coalitions." His book, *Chain of Change* concludes:

> If as a community we are prepared to lead others through the experience of learning to cooperate, dealing honestly with painful prejudices and tensions built into this society, and learning to bend enough in times of need so that the whole is more flexible and resilient, we will be able to do more than control our own community. We will be able to influence larger sections of the city, bringing together an array of potential allies.
>
> Further movement within the system around us, so laden with conflict-producing tensions, cannot happen without an alliance. People must come together, moving out of their isolation, to challenge conditions which exploit us.

What we have described [in this recent history of Boston] is changing relationships, between people of color and white folks; between have-nots and have-a-lots; between men and women. While all these changes have been going on within the community of color, similar changes have been occurring to many other groups....

The chain of change is still being forged.[60]

Acknowledgements: I would like to thank the people who talked with me about this article: Henry Allen, Allen Hunter, James Jennings, Lew Finfer, Bill Fletcher, Martin Gopen, Charlotte Ryan, Art Standley, and Jim Tramel. Thanks also to RA editors Linda Gordon and Jim O'Brien for their help.

Notes

1. *Time,* October 10, 1983, p. 30.
2. *Ibid.*
3. For a further comparison of these two sections of Boston and explanation for the South End's tolerance, see James Green, "Learning from the South End's Ethnic Tradition," *Boston Phoenix,* June 24, 1975.
4. David Nyhan, "Populism was the big victor in this election," *Boston Globe,* October 13, 1983, p. 19.
5. *Ibid.* and p. 30.
6. "Flynn for Mayor," *Boston Globe,* November 8, 1983, p. 17. For an endorsement of Flynn by a socialist supporter, see Peter Dreier, "A Choice for a Change," *In These Times,* September 7, 1983 and for responses by King supporters, see letter from Bob Keough, *ibid.,* September 21, 1983 and James Jennings, "A New Kind of Black Politics," *ibid.,* October 5, 1983, p. 15. Jennings confronted the pragmatic argument that King could not win in Boston and that support for him would be wasted. He described it as a "subtle racist position."
7. *Boston Globe,* November 16, 1983, pp. 1, 34.
8. King's 20 percent can also be compared to the 26 percent of the white vote gained in Philadelphia by Wilson Goode, a black candidate considered far more "acceptable" to white voters because of his moderate positions and because he had been preceded by six previous black mayoral candidates. *Boston Globe,* November 16, 1983, p. 3, and Robert A. Jordan, "King's Defeat and the Racial Hurdle," *ibid.* November 17, 1983, p. 29. J.D. Nelson, King's campaign manager, thought the candidate had been "hurt badly" among white voters by his "apparently unintentional statement" that the late Catholic Cardinal had made anti-Semitic remarks. *Ibid.,* November 16, 1983, p. 34. Charles Stith, an activist black minister close to King, also thought that this "faux pas," as well as controversial comments favorable to Fidel Castro and Yassir Arafat, cost the candidate white Catholic votes.
9. *Boston Globe,* November 16, 1983, p. 1.

10. The term "pro-growth coalition" is from John H. Mollenkopf, "The Post-War Politics of Urban Development," in William K. Tabb and Larry Sawers, eds., *Marxism and the Metropolis*, Oxford University Press, New York, 1978, pp. 117-53. This article also offers an excellent analysis of post-war politics in Boston.
11. Quoted in Daniel Golden and David Mehegan, "Changing the Heart of the City," *Boston Globe Magazine*, September 18, 1983, p. 22.
12. Mollenkopf, "The Post-War Politics of Urban Development," p. 123, 137.
13. On the old West End, see Herbert Gans, *The Urban Villagers*, The Free Press, New York, 1962, and Mare Fried, *The World of the Urban Working Class*, Harvard University Press, Cambridge, 1973.
14. Mollenkopf, "The Post-War Politics of Urban Development," pp. 137-38.
15. Much of this history of the busing conflict is drawn from Jim Green and Allen Hunter, "Racism and Busing in Boston," *Radical America* Vol. 8, No, 6. Nov.-Dec., 1974, pp. 1-32, reprinted in Tabb and Sawers, *Marxism and the Metropolis*, pp. 27-96.
16. Mel King, *Chain of Change: Struggles for Black Community Development*, South End Press, Boston, 1981, pp. 32-34.
17. Peter Schrag, *Village School Downtown, Boston Schools, Boston Politics*, Beacon Press, Boston, 1967, p. 13, 18-20.
18. King, *Chain of Change*, pp. 34-46, 85-94.
19. *Ibid.*, pp. 95-127.
20. James Jennings, "Black Politics in Boston, 1900-1975," unpublished manuscript.
21. King, *Chain of Change*, pp. 23-24.
22. *Ibid.*, preface, pp. xxv-viii.
23. James Jennings, "Boston Machinism and Black Politics," unpublished manuscript.
24. Green and Hunter, "Racism and Busing in Boston," pp. 15-19 and King, *Chain of Change*, pp. 155-169.
25. *Ibid.*, pp. 163-164.
26. *Ibid.*
27. Jill Nelson-Ricks, "Rainbow Politics: Mel King Boston Dream," *Village Voice*, October 25, 1983, pp. 22-24.
28. "Racism and Busing in Boston: Comments and Criticisms," *Radical America*, Vol. 9, No. 3, May-June 1975, pp. 88-89.
29. Mollenkopf, "The Post-War Politics of Urban Development," p. 141, and Golden and Mehegan, "Changing the Heart of the City," p. 68.
30. Ann Kirchheimer, "The Haves and Have-Nots Fight Over the South End," *Boston Globe*, April 30, 1974, p. 34.
31. Mollenkopf, "The Post-War Politics of Urban Development," pp. 141, 144.
32. King, *Chain of Change*, p. 216.
33. Jennings, "Boston Machinism and Black Politics," and "The Black Voter in Boston," unpublished manuscripts. Thanks to James Jennings for allowing the author to read his unpublished work.

34. King, *Chain of Change,* pp. 215-218.
35. *Ibid.* pp. 219-220.
36. *Ibid.* pp. 219-220.
37. Jennings, "A New Kind of Black Politics," p. 15.
38. King, *Chain of Change,* pp. 221-223.
39. *Ibid.* pp. 223-224.
40. *Boston Globe,* January 29, 1984, p. 59.
41. King, *Chain of Change,* pp. 169-184.
42. *Ibid.* pp. 185-194.
43. Golden and Mehegan, "Changing the Heart of the City," p. 74.
44. Jim Green, "The destruction of the South End Lodging House," *South End Community News,* Summer 1974.
45. Golden and Mehegan, "Changing the Heart of the City," 69-70, 72, 74.
46. *Ibid.* p. 85.
47. King, *Chain of Change,* pp. 207-20.
48. See *Langley Keyes, The Rehabilitation Planning Game,* Cambridge, M.I.T. Press, 1969.
49. Joe Klein, "The Rise and Fall of The People First," *Real Paper,* October 10, 1973, pp. 4-5, 11-15.
50. Howard Husock, "Getting Their Fair Share," *Boston Globe Magazine,* June 14, 1981, pp. 10, 28, 33.
51. Quote on Fair Share from Harry Boyte, *The Backyard Revolution: Understanding the New Citizen Movement,* Temple University Press, Philadelphia, 1980, p. 98. For a criticism of Boyte's favorable view of Fair Share organizing, see Frank Ackerman, "The Melting Snowball: Limits of the 'New Populism' in Practice," *Socialist Review* 35, September-October, 1977, pp. 113-124 and for Boyte's response, see *Ibid.,* pp. 125-128.
52. Husock, "Getting Their Fair Share," p. 42.
53. *Boston Globe,* October 16, 1983, Section A, p. 25.
54. These points are developed in James Green, "King, Flynn and Populism," *Boston Globe,* October 28, 1983, p. 19.
55. Quotes from Lawrence Goodwyn, *The Populist Moment,* New York: Oxford University Press, 1978, p. 121. Though Goodwyn sees the ways in which populist economism caused problems for black farmers, he does not fault the movement for failing to address racism within its own ranks, perhaps because he believes the Southern white populists were not aware of "their own participation in a caste system" that subjugated blacks. The problems resulting from the failure of radicals and reformers to confront racism within their own movements or within society generally are discussed in Robert Allen, *Reluctant Reformers,* Garden City, N.Y., Anchor, 1975. The tragedy of Tom Watson's shift from populism to racism, anti-Semitism and anti-radicalism is epically described in C. Vann Woodward, *Tom Watson, Agrarian Rebel,* Oxford University Press, New York, 1983.
56. For a more general discussion of these approaches to equality see William Ryan, *Equality,* Basic Books, New York, 1982.
57. For a discussion of the dual nature of this consciousness about welfare,

based on interviews with Boston workers, see Richard Sennett and Jonathan Cobb, *The Hidden Injuries of Class*, Alfred A. Knopf, New York, 1972, pp. 136-137.
  58. Flynn's social democratic supporters argued that he was a better coalition builder than King and better able to heal the city's "social, economic *and racial* wounds" (emphasis added). Peter Dreier and Kevin Sidel, "Building a Governing Coalition," *Boston Globe*, November 5, 1983, p. 15. As mayor, Flynn has agreed to follow through the affirmative action hiring quotas at Copley Place initially proposed and developed by Mel King and his supporters, he has visited a black family attacked by white youths and has pleaded for racial calm in a newly desegregated Charlestown housing project. But people of color have not received their proportionate share of appointments, at any level, in Flynn's City Hall. Flynn's identification with Curley's personal style of populism would be very threatening if carried too far. Curley showed gross favoritism in hiring, and when confronted with massive joblessness during the depression, he failed to meet the crisis and became a notorious red-baiter. He also discouraged independent movements like the CIO, to keep workers dependent on his personal political organization. See James R. Green and Hugh Carter Donahue, *Boston's Workers: A Labor History*, Boston Public Library, Boston, 1979, pp. 106-111.
  59. King, *Chain of Change*, p. 169.
  60. *Ibid.*, p. 260.

VII
What's Black, White and Racist All Over?
William E. Alberts

Mel King did not lose Boston's 1983 mayoral election simply to Raymond Flynn. He lost it to certain of the city's powerful white-owned media, which controlled the information voters received and thus helped to manipulate their opinions and decisions about the candidates. Understanding how and why these particular media influenced voters' thinking and thus orchestrated Mel King's defeat has important implications for the next mayoral election—and for the presidential campaign and Rev. Jesse Jackson's candidacy as well. Boston's mayoral election also reveals the powerful role the media play in general in influencing people's thoughts, beliefs and behavior, in defining for people the nature of their problems and what and who are needed to protect their interests.

The campaign to stop Mel King from becoming mayor of Boston began long before he and Flynn won in the preliminary. *The Boston Globe* played a primary role.

Early on *The Globe* began telling its readers that there was no difference between King and Flynn. Columnist David Nyhan stated, "Flynn and Mel King are duking it out for the vote of the dispossessed, the little guy, the renter or three-decker owner who's felt lost in the Kevin White shuffle." (August 28, 1983, page A21). Associate editor Ian Menzies wrote, "Flynn and King, with emphasis on the little guy, access, housing and neighborhoods, come closest to a shared philosophy..." (Sept. 22, 1983, page 33). Columnist Robert L. Turner concluded, "They nominated two men with many similar qualities—particularly concern for the poor, for individual problems and neighborhood development, and for trying to get the city to pull together." (*Boston Globe Magazine,* November 13, 1983, page 62). Associate editor Robert Healy even assumed, "For those who were left behind in the rebirth movement of the city, there are two candidates, Flynn and Mel King. If the polls are anywhere near accurate, it is Flynn rather than King who is becoming the candidate of those who were left behind." (Aug. 17, 1983, page 23).

Many of those dispossessed and left behind are people of color. The public records of King and Flynn toward them are vastly different and provided a major comparison for the voters. This critical comparison was never made. In fact, Flynn's greatest weakness—his regressive record on racism—not only was laid to rest by *The Boston Globe;* it was resurrected as a strong point.

Healy stated, "... in a city which has at times been torn by strife, Flynn is a healer. He has demonstrated he can deal with the race issue." (Aug. 17, 1983, page 23). Nyhan matter-of-factly declared, "Flynn's a healer on the race issue." (Aug. 28, 1983, page A 21). Menzies wrote, "Both (Flynn and King) claim to be healers, men who could lower racial tensions in a still racially-tense city, and both have credentials to prove it. Two men, one black, one white, running on a platform of racial peace." (Sept. 22, 1983, page 33). None of the three presented any evidence to support their assertion that Flynn is a racial healer.

A classic example of this unsubstantiated assertion is provided by columnists Jack Germond and Jules Witcover, who offered to voters the following quote about Flynn from an authoritative source whom they never identify: "'He's a good politician, a real outside player,' says an astute professional aligned with another candidate. And as for the busing issue, 'It isn't there. He doesn't have a racist bone in his body.'" (*The Boston Globe,* Aug. 10, 1983, page 19). Germond and Witcover quote their same authoritative anonymous source in another *Globe* column two months later: "'You can't make it stick that Ray Flynn is a racist,' says a liberal in another camp. 'Ray hasn't got a racist bone in his body and people know that.'" (Oct. 15, 1983, page 19). Germond and Witcover are *Baltimore Sun-employed and Washington-based* syndicated columnists.

The Boston Globe's campaign to present Flynn as a racial healer to the voters is seen in its making much of the one and only endorsement Flynn received from a black minister. Germond and Witcover's August 10 column is captioned "Flynn finds support in an unexpected

What's Black, White and Racist? 139

place," and begins with, "Ray Flynn does not find it all that unusual that he has been endorsed for mayor by the pastor of the church in Roxbury with the largest black congregation in Boston." A month earlier *Globe* reporter Charles Kennedy's piece called "A relaxed Flynn feels the momentum" states, "Flynn said one highlight of his campaign came Sunday when he was endorsed by Rev. R. D. Kelley, minister for the past 40 years at St. John the Baptist Missionary Church, Roxbury. The predominantly black congregation has 3300 members. During a sermon to 600 persons at the church Sunday Kelley said Flynn 'has been our friend' and can 'bring this city together'."[1] (July 12, 1983, page 16).

Compare the attention *The Globe* gave to this lone black minister's endorsement of Flynn with its coverage of the endorsement Mel King received from many black and white and Latino religious leaders. When Chicago Mayor Harold Washington came to Boston last August, before the preliminary, to endorse Mel King's candidacy, *The Globe* reported in passing, "At St. Mark's Church on Townsend Street, Roxbury, Washington participated in an interracial, interdenominational assembly where 70 members of the clergy endorsed King." (Aug. 8, 1983, page 16). *Globe* readers were not informed that 30 of these 70 religious leaders were black clergy representing a great many of Boston's black population.

The 70 religious leaders' endorsement of Mel King was not included in columnist Robert L. Turner's opposite ed. piece on "Boston liberals divided in mayor's race," in which he listed liberal groups endorsing various candidates. (Aug. 23, 1983, page 11). The omission led this writer to state in a letter to Turner, "During the extensive racial violence in the fall of 1979, which included the tragic shooting of Darryl Williams, *Boston Globe* editorials strongly criticized religious leaders for not speaking out against the violence, and stressed the importance of their role in dealing with Boston's racial problems. Seventy religious leaders endorse Mel King for mayor with a powerful statement, and the very newspaper that had pleaded for religious leadership in response to such a critical city-wide problem now has a hard time even recognizing the endorsement of Mel King by such a large group of interracial and ecumenical religious leaders."

This letter appeared to help lead Turner to write a column, which focused on the separation of church and state and the participation of clergy in politics. The column included a reference to the endorsement of Mel King by the 70 religious leaders. But it did not state any of the critical reasons why they believe King was the one candidate uniquely qualified to set such a powerful example of inclusiveness that the diversity of Boston's citizens would indeed be a source of strength rather than strife. It took five weeks for *The Globe* to report that King received the endorsement of so many black, white and Latino religious leaders, and even then it did not print any of the reasons for their endorsement. King ended up with well over 100 such endorsements.

The day before the November 15th election, *four months* after Rev. Kelley's endorsement of Flynn, *The Boston Herald* carried a page 3 story called "Black pastor backs Flynn." The story began, "Mayoral candidate Ray Flynn captured a key endorsement in the black community *yesterday* (italics added) by winning the backing of Rev. Rafe D. Kelley, the pastor of Boston's largest black congregation. 'It shows the city is finally coming together,' said Flynn after receiving the endorsement before some 100 black voters at St. John's Missionary Baptist Church in Roxbury." The story also featured a large photograph of Flynn and a black youngster sitting in pews next to and smiling at each other.

When the 70 black, white and Latino religious leaders endorsed Mel King's candidacy the day (August 7) Chicago Mayor Harold Washington endorsed him, *The Boston Herald*'s coverage did not even mention the religious leaders' endorsement.

The Boston Globe's role in helping to orchestrate Flynn's election is seen in its treatment of his actual record on racial issues. It is here especially that his greatest weakness is "transformed" into a source of strength.

Flynn was a prominent leader of Boston's so-called "anti-busing" forces. South Boston's state representative from 1971 through 1979, he was militantly opposed to court-ordered busing, begun in 1974, to achieve racial desegregation of the city's public schools. He not only filed a bill in 1975 that would have abolished compulsory school attendance in Massachusetts; in 1974 he was quoted as playing a major role in the boycott of South Boston schools. It was this role that led mayoral candidate Robert Kiley, then a deputy mayor and coordinator of public safety, to charge in a televised candidates' debate that Flynn was "on the wrong side of police lines."

What's Black, White and Racist? 141

Three days after the debate, in an August 20 column called "Flynn, then and now," deputy editor of the *Globe* editorial page Kirk Scharfenberg wrote, "All hail to Robert Kiley's virtue"; pointed out Kiley is fortunate enough to afford to send his child to a private school; stated, "What cannot be hailed is Kiley's apparent insensitivity to the very real class issues in the city"; and added, "Flynn was defending, however inappropriate his tactics, the interests of those who felt their children were trapped in Boston's schools."

Scharfenberg continued, "Kiley's assertion that he faced Flynn across police lines certainly fostered the inaccurate notion that Flynn was out there throwing rocks at passing buses. Not only is that untrue by all accounts, but, according to reporters who covered the sad events of the early days of busing, Flynn was less a screaming opponent of busing than many other prominent South Boston politicians. His opposition put him on the 'same side' as some violent bigots. But many saw him as a moderating force; his fault, others say, was that he was ambiguous."

According to Scharfenberg, those "who are inclined to support Flynn—and I am one—have to weigh whether Flynn has grown in the last few years, not only on educational issues but, notably, on racial issues and women's issues as well. A candidate's past record is one important measure by which to judge him. Surely, however, it is better to have been wrong yesterday and right today than the reverse."

And he left the reader with, "In my view, the ability to reach out from the air-conditioned mayor's suite at city hall across lines of both class and race—to understand genuinely the fears and hopes of those left out, to place an unremitting emphasis on the needs of the poor and near poor of the city—is the quality most needed in Boston's next mayor. It may help to have been there."

Here again no proof was provided to support the contention that Flynn "has grown ... notably, on racial issues and women's issues." The logic that "it is better to have been wrong yesterday and right today" is presented without any evidence to substantiate the implication that Flynn was "right today." The reasoning that "the ability to reach ... across both lines of class and race" is related, in Flynn's case somehow, to "it may help to have been there," is offered without furnishing any documentation or accurate picture of where Flynn actually had been. For certain *Globe* columnists, it is as if saying it makes it so—which reveals far more about where *The Boston Globe* is coming from than where Raymond Flynn has been—and is now.

Instead of presenting examples of Flynn's "ability to reach... across both lines of class and race," Scharfenberg actually used "the very real class issues in the city" to justify the racism of "those who felt their children were trapped in Boston schools."

Scharfenberg used classism to justify racism: the oppression of white persons by white persons to justify the racism of both groups toward people of color. The racism of classism: an ironic twist that played a key role in helping to influence the outcome of the election.

Scharfenberg effectively exorcised Flynn's record from Flynn's candidacy for mayor. He also put would-be critics of Flynn's involvement in racial problems on notice that they risked the same sarcastic and stinging treatment *The Globe* gave Kiley.

Scharfenberg's message was reinforced two days later by Mike Barnicle's column which refuted Kiley's criticism of Flynn. Barnicle described a personal encounter with Flynn, who was standing on a South Boston street corner, "urging calm... drenched with perspiration and looked as if he had not slept in a week... trying to push kids from the corner," saying, "'Get the... outta' here... If you're not going inside the school, go the... home.'"

Barnicle also made it a point to inform readers that Kiley had "worked quite diligently with men named Richard Helms and William Colby in the Central Intelligence Agency. During Kiley's time of employment his superiors conducted—among other things—something called Operation Phoenix... a program of planned assassinations that resulted in the deaths of many, many Vietnamese nationals, a program excused by all because it fell under the heading of war 'effort'."

Barnicle ended with, "Right now the schools are largely a proposition of the non-white poor. Busing brought racism and fear and white flight from classrooms... In 1975 Ray Flynn was indeed out on the street. He was there because the people he represents don't measure assets by wealth: they measure them by birthdays and graduations."

The Globe's continuing "transformation" of Flynn's record on racial issues followed candidate David Finnegan's charge that Flynn used a "racist" strategy in passing out one set of flyers, showing him with whites only, in predominantly white sections of Dorchester and another set, picturing him almost exclusively with blacks, in mainly black sections. In a column called "The Flynn-Finnegan donnybrook," associate editor Healey wrote of Flynn's campaign strategy, "It was a mistake. But to know Ray Flynn is to know it was not racist. Flynn has made mistakes in the past. The know-nothing legislation that came out of the busing situation in Boston was not his finest hour. But while a lot of people were ducking, Ray Flynn was a peacemaker in one of Boston's darkest and most vicious hours, when the poor were fighting the poor. In those days in the mid 1970's, Ray Flynn was considered an upstart by the followers of Louise Day Hicks and John Kerrigan because the real leaders of the anti-busing movement started all the fights for political advantage and then walked away from them. Flynn never walked away." (Oct. 5, 1983, page 19).

The Globe's introduction into the mayoral campaign of the testimony of a key, authoritatively positioned educator helped to solidify the newspaper's "transformation" of Flynn's record on racial issues. In a column on "Flynn devious? His record says 'no,'" Robert Turner wrote, "One of the most strongly felt testaments to Flynn's commitment comes from a source that may be surprising to some: South Boston High School Headmaster Jerome Winegar. When Winegar arrived in 1976 most Boston politicians ignored or ducked him. But Flynn, protesting his continued opposition to busing all the while, offered to help within the school. 'Whenever there was a serious problem in the school, I would always call him, and within 30 or 40 minutes he was on the property,' Winegar said last week in an interview. 'He would walk the halls, he would sit in the cafeteria, he would talk with black kids or with white kids. He did whatever would help. He's an honest guy; I've learned that I can depend on him.'" (Sept. 25, 1983, page 81).

Following the preliminary, Flynn himself relied heavily on Winegar's assumed authoritative testimony in his campaign to defeat Mel King and become mayor. At a November 6 debate, sponsored by a group of interracial religious leaders, Flynn said, "During the school desegregation period, there was one person during the whole period of time that was brought in by the courts, not all that well accepted, but brought in ... to make sure that the desegregation order was implemented and that public safety in education was conducted—that was the headmaster of South Boston High School. Many people from the media have gone to the headmaster of South Boston High School and asked what kind of role was played by various political figures in the city. The headmaster ... clearly states that of all the people in the city who held public office Ray Flynn was the person who provided the most stable, positive influence. Ray Flynn went into the classrooms, and broke up fights; he spoke to blacks, he spoke to whites. He provided the leadership that was necessary. And I'm very, very proud of that. Anybody here, who wants to, particularly the media could pick up the phone and call Mr. Winegar, and I'm sure he would be very happy to make a comment on it. He was the person who best understands the situation going on in the schools at that time. My record is very clear; again, I'm proud of it. I was there, I was accessible. I provided the moral leadership, the political leadership this city needed. I was there, open, dealt with the problem, which was a very difficult problem in 1974. Looking back at it again I refuse to allow that issue or any other issue to divide this city."

Ray Flynn was there in 1974, but South Boston High School Headmaster Jerome Winegar was not there. *He did not arrive until 1976.*

Ray Flynn was there in 1974, but he did not provide "the moral (and) political leadership this city needed." Not only did he allow that issue to divide the city; he played a key inflammatory role in dividing the city and helping to disrupt the education of children and young people—the record speaks for itself. *The Boston Globe's* record contradicts its own and other media's attempts, during the mayoral campaign, to portray Mel King and Raymond Flynn as similar and Flynn as a "peacemaker" and "healer on the race issue."

The first buses carrying black students to South Boston High School in 1974 were stoned; nine black students and a school bus monitor were injured; white students and parents joined in a planned walkout and boycott of the schools; and a large demonstration at South Boston High School was punctuated by all sorts of racial slurs against black students and their families.

Then South Boston State Representative Ray Flynn, described as one of the "leaders of Boston's anti-busing movement," was there in 1974, and was quoted by *The Boston Globe* itself (Sept. 13, 1974, page 3) as saying that "the anti-busing organization ROAR (Restore Our Alienated Rights) would try to get exemptions from the busing court order for younger children and also would test the compulsory school attendance laws in the court. 'If those measures don't work, *we* [italics added] may vote to extend the boycott,' Flynn said." *Globe* columnists' efforts to dissociate Flynn from more militant anti-busing

What's Black, White and Racist? 145

leaders is not supported by this and other references to his behavior.

Flynn was reported to be furious over the curfew imposed in South Boston and the extra amount of police protection there: "Flynn likened police activities and the imposed curfew yesterday to the Soviet takeover of Budapest," charged the police " 'take our schools, now they take our streets.'" He called it " 'the most degrading thing to South Boston... an outrage and the most important thing to discuss with (Mayor Kevin White),'" and blamed police presence for the violence in saying, " 'When the police show up here in riot gear, horses and dogs, word gets around South Boston that something big is happening at South Boston High School. That's when all the trouble starts.'" (*Boston Evening Globe*, Sept. 13, 1974, page 3; *The Boston Globe*, Sept. 14, 1974, pages 1 and 4).

Rep. Flynn was not portrayed as a "peacemaker" providing "stable ... positive... moral leadership." He was not quoted in *The Globe* stories as condemning and lamenting the stoning and injuring of the nine black students and the monitor and the many racist slurs against black persons.

Jerome Winegar was not there to observe the kind of leadership role Ray Flynn played. And when Winegar did arrive in 1976, Rep. Flynn's leadership role in response to Winegar himself was not "stable" and "positive." A *South Boston Tribune* story (April 22, page 12), called "Patronage The Game In Boston, Not Education, Says Rep. Flynn," began with, " 'The people of Boston have not been told the real truth why the team of Mario Fantini and Jerome Winegar have been employed by the Boston School Department,' emphatically stated Rep. Raymond L. Flynn. 'This is no longer a question of busing and desegregation,' said Flynn, 'the name of the game is patronage and power. It's blatantly obvious that these men are not here to improve our children's education, but to ram a program down the throats of the parents and citizens of Boston. A program which is certain to bring more chaos and confusion to Boston,' said Rep. Flynn. 'As usual patronage continues to dominate and manipulate our city and our children's education,' said Rep. Flynn."

Flynn's condemnation of Winegar's appointment as headmaster of South Boston High School followed another group's objections to the selection of Winegar. Two weeks before Flynn's statement the *South Boston Tribune* (April 8, pages 1 and 3) reported, "The South Boston High School Home and School Association has made public, through its president, James M. Kelly, its objections to the selection of Jerome Winegar as headmaster of the high school." Kelly stated that Winegar was "unacceptable for three reasons: '1 . . . Education has taken a back seat to social programs. Because of the lack of discipline, there are still racial problems [in the junior high school where he had been headmaster]. 2. Mr. Winegar has admitted his affiliation with the National Association for the Advancement of Colored People. Behind every court order in this country whether it be forced busing, Affirmative Action programs, or quota systems, lies the hands of the National Association for the Advancement of Colored People. 3. Mr. Winegar supports the American Civil Liberties Union . . . a very patriotic sounding organization [which] supports people and causes that are detrimental to this country. Under the guise of protecting the Constitution, the American Civil Liberties Union are [sic] promoting moral decay. Some of their causes include: Prisoners rights . . . Anti-religion . . . Abortion . . . Promote pornography. In summary they are Anti-God, Anti-Law enforcement, and Anti-American.'"

Portraying Flynn as a "peacemaker in one of Boston's darkest and most vicious hours, when the poor were fighting the poor,"reveals a tragic lack of investigative journalism. One such dark and vicious hour began in April of 1976 when black attorney Theodore Landsmark was brutally assaulted on City Hall Plaza by several members of a group of about 250 South Boston and Charlestown high school "anti-busing" student protesters, the primary assault weapon being the flagpole bearing an American flag, wielded by a South Boston student. Mel King's response was to join in urging his legislative colleagues to approve a resolution condemning the conduct of the assailants, saying, "'The issue is not black and white, but right and wrong. The seed of fascist behavior was exemplified by what went on in Boston yesterday. This resolution is the first step to access of all public facilities for people of color in Boston.' . . . King said the racial climate in Boston has gotten so bad that 'we are a people who no longer go to work in certain sections of the city. We have given up jobs for fear of life and limb.'" King also told the legislators, "If you are silent, you are saying (to any of their constituents), 'You have a license to brutalize.'" (*The Boston Globe*, April 7, 1976, page 6).

No comment by South Boston State Rep. Raymond Flynn was quoted in this extensive *Boston Globe* piece. Nor did any statement from Flynn regarding the vicious beating of Landsmark appear in the

What's Black, White and Racist? 147

South Boston Tribune, which regularly carried his constant attacks against court-ordered busing. (*The Tribune* did not even carry a story about Landsmark's beating.)

Two weeks later Richard Poleet, a white service station mechanic, was viciously beaten and stoned into unconsciousness in Roxbury by a gang of 15 to 20 black youths. Flynn's outrage was published as a front-page story called "Streets Made Battleground by Busing Order, Flynn Says," in the April 22 *South Boston Tribune*: "Representative Raymond L. Flynn expressed outrage at Monday night's unprovoked and senseless beating of a white man by a gang of between 15 and 20 black youths in the Roxbury section of Boston. 'I wonder if the Boston media will respond with the same outrage as with the beating at City Hall Plaza of Atty. Theodore Landsmark just two weeks ago,' said Flynn. 'The streets of Boston have become a virtual battleground since the forced school busing court order of Federal District Judge W. Arthur Garrity, Jr.,' said Rep. Flynn. 'It is absolutely amazing what one court decision can do to race relations in the city of Boston.'"

This *South Boston Tribune* story also reported, "The Boston lawmaker introduced a Resolution in the Massachusetts House of Representatives on Tuesday, deploring the senseless beating of the Jamaica Plain man in the streets of Roxbury, and called on the U.S. Justice Department to prosecute the offenders of the Patriots Day beating to the full extent of the law. The House adopted the Resolution unanimously."

Flynn's stating of whether the Boston media would respond with the same outrage to Poleet's beating as to Landsmark's was carried in the April 20 *Boston Globe*.

Mel King also condemned the vicious beating of Poleet, and called for much more. "'I most certainly insist that the same approach that has been taken against white violence be taken in this and any other instance of violence.'" (*The Boston Globe*, April 21, 1976, page 1). He then "called for a joint statement by black and white community leaders deploring the beating. 'What's more important is that people with differences over busing have to come together and say they have no differences on the issues of violence and safety in the streets.'" (*Ibid.*, page 12).

During the severe overt racial violence in 1976, 3 of the 28 members of the Boston delegation to the Massachusetts House of Representatives refused to sign a joint statement deploring the acts of violence. Raymond Flynn was one of the three. "'The one thing killing this city more than anything else is violence,' the statement said. 'To some of us,' it continued, 'we see it springing from an overzealous, rigid and uncompromising federal judge and federal officials out of touch with reality. To others, we see it as an extension of a long history of unequal opportunity in schools, housing, jobs and economic opportunity, and a continued unwillingness to see that system changed.'" (*The Boston Herald*, April 22, page 8).

Flynn and fellow South Boston Representative Michael Flaherty released their own statement. In a piece called "Flynn, Flaherty blame Garrity busing order," *The Boston Herald* (April 23, page 8) reported, "While deploring the violence plaguing Boston, they emphasized, however, 'it does no good to merely state that we are experiencing turmoil and chaos unless we are willing to talk about the causes. SENSIBLE men,' they asserted, 'know that the problems of violence are not going to go away by mere pleas for calm while the storm threatens to engulf us all and destroy our great city.' Flynn and Flaherty issued their statement after earlier refusing to join 25 other Boston legislators in signing a statement that also condemned the violence but pointed out there was disagreement over the causes. The earlier statement said some legislators believe the violence is caused by Garrity's 'rigid and uncompromising' position while other[s] link it to a 'long history of unequal opportunity' in schools, housing, and jobs. 'Busing has divided this city,' Flynn and Flaherty said... Good men are outraged at the escalation of violence, wise men will recognize the failure of busing, and courageous men will admit the mistakes of two years and resolve to do something about them.'" Several days later: "Rep. Flynn concluded, 'We must put an end to busing or busing will put an end to our city.'" (*South Boston Tribune*, June 3, 1976, page 3).

These statements and actions occurred at the very time Jerome Winegar, as Flynn said during the campaign, "was brought in by the courts to make sure that the desegregation order was implemented and that public safety in education was conducted."

South Boston High School Headmaster Jerome Winegar showed up in *The Boston Globe* during the mayoral campaign as saying that Flynn came to South Boston High School when called and acted as a peacemaker between white and black students. In 1979 and 1980 Winegar was quoted as saying something quite different, which was not reported during the campaign by *The Boston Globe* and certain other white-controlled media.

In 1979 three buses carrying black students to South Boston High School were "ambushed" by 15 white students, "who hurled rocks, bricks and steel bolts, three-to-four inches in length at the windows." Boston police and the U.S. Justice Department said the brutal attack was 'organized' and 'planned'... Authorities said it was the first major racial incident this school year." (*The Boston Herald*, September 19, 1979, page A3). An October 23 *Boston Globe* story states that "Boston Police Supt. John Doyle said yesterday that he now believes there 'definitely' has been adult involvement behind recent disturbances and protests by students in the city's public schools... Last month Doyle had said he knew of 'no evidence' of adults being involved in the Sept. 18 stoning of school buses in South Boston, which in retrospect is seen as the first chain of racial incidents of the current school year. Yesterday, however, he confirmed that four teams of detectives have been assigned to an investigation of that stoning and of subsequent incidents which have involved both black and white students in schools across the city." (page 14).

The lack of response of political leaders to the stoning of the buses and other disturbances led South Boston High School Headmaster Jerome Winegar to sharply criticize the city's political leadership. In a front-page story called "Winegar hits politicians for silence in S. Boston," he was quoted as charging, "I can't believe that *not a single politician or government leader* [italics added] has spoken out in any way.[3] The folks who are in charge of this city don't seem to care what happens here.... Maybe they hope this school will fall into the ocean." (*The Boston Globe*, city edition, September 20, 1979, pages 1 and 2). Winegar believed the "racial violence in and around the city schools was 'orchestrated by haters who have more control over the kids than we do.'" (*The Boston Herald*, October 24, 1979, page 1). He also was quoted as saying of the stoning of the buses in South Boston, "'On Friday night, Sept. 14, the South Boston Information Center had an anti-busing rally on the steps of the high school. The following Tuesday, the buses with black kids on them were stoned by the masked white kids. It was probably the most vicious single incident since I've been here. And when *no* [italics added] city leader spoke out to say those kinds of things are wrong, their silence only supported the kids. Their silence made cowards of us all.'" (*Ibid.*) Ten days later a more vicious incident occurred: Darryl Williams, a black 15-year-old Jamaica Plain High School football player, was critically wounded by one of three white youths while standing on the Charlestown High School football field.

One city leader not only spoke out, but led 1,000 people of color and white persons of all ages in an orderly, peaceful walk to bring Boston's serious racial problems to the attention of Pope John Paul II when he visited our city three days after the Williams youth was shot. That leader was Mel King—who also took another positive initiative. He joined with concerned clergy in asking Cardinal Humberto Medeiros to provide leadership in dealing with the racial strife threatening to tear our city apart. That joint effort led the late Cardinal Medeiros to initiate a series of meetings among black and white community leaders and clergy which resulted in the creation of the city-wide "Covenant of Justice, Equity and Harmony."

In 1980 extensive racial violence and walkouts returned to South Boston and other schools. The violence and other disruptions were so severe that Winegar again made the same criticism of political leaders: "I have the same criticisms of the city I always have. There's no real leadership to stop this stuff. Have you ever heard *anybody* [italics added] say it's terrible? That only happens if somebody gets shot." (*The Boston Globe*, September 13, 1980, page 14).

Mel King had been saying it was terrible long before Winegar came to Boston. And the lack of white political leadership was lamented publically long before Winegar became critical of it.

In the fall of 1973, extensive racial violence (receiving national headlines) gripped Boston for three weeks, and included the murders of two white and one black persons and considerable fighting between white and black students in South Boston, Dorchester and Jamaica Plain. A major concern was the lack of political leadership in response to the widespread violence. *The Boston Globe* published a lengthy front-page piece called "Hub leaders tread softly on racial issues," the focus being that "no one in power either on Beacon Hill or in City Hall was coming forward with plans or programs to steer the city sharply away from racial confrontation..." (October 14, 1973, pages 1 and 2).

But one (and only one) of the 1983 mayoral candidates did come forward and address the issues, and the same *Globe* story quoted him. "Said State Rep. Mel King of the South End, a leader of the legislative black caucus: 'Part of the problem is resources and program development, but part of it is also the fact that there isn't positive white leadership who will stand up and be counted. . . . There has . . . to be some admission on the part of the mayor or whatever white leadership you do find in the city that there is a real problem in lots of places, and I'm talking about South Boston, and Charlestown, Jamaica Plain and Dorchester. It's crucial in terms of people living in really hostile relationships. You can't get people talking to each other when there's a denial that this sort of problem exists, which is not to say that there aren't people co-existing and working together.'"

In another newspaper again it was Mel King alone who spoke out and with real clarity about the violence and the underlying issues of schools, housing, jobs, neighborhood services, and community participation in crime prevention. And he concluded with a positive vision that embraced white persons and people of color alike: "Why do we overlook the opportunities. There is work for everyone: think of the housing that needs to be built, the clean-up that is needed across the city, the wasteland of I-95 that needs to be rebuilt and revitalized. Park Plaza is not the answer, but there are numerous other good answers right before our eyes. People want to stay and make our city work—city hall has thousands of inquiries about the proposed homesteading in the city. We must unite in encouraging people—black and white—who want to stay and build. Their vitality will attract others and provide a model for all of us who want to solve our problems." (*The Boston Ledger*, October 12, 1973, pages 6 and 31).

South Boston High School Headmaster Winegar, the very person used in the mayoral campaign to give Flynn desperately needed credibility on racial issues, also contradicted Flynn's continuing position on the education of Boston's children and young people. Flynn repeatedly presented his so-called "anti-busing" position during the campaign: "I never felt one minute that busing was going to be productive for improving the quality of education in Boston; it was educationally counterproductive for this city." (*The Boston Globe*, April 15, 1983, page 17).

In 1980 Jerome Winegar was quoted as telling a thousand people at a racial convocation for Boston at Trinity Church that South Boston High and other inner city schools in pre-desegregation days were a "'travesty of public education' whose students were 'programmed for failure,'" "that only through court-ordered desegregation at South Boston High School in 1974 was an 'irrelevant, unsound and outdated educational system' exposed. And only because of the attention focused on that school were administrators able to get 'carte blanche to revamp the whole system.'" And it also was noted by a colleague of Winegar's that "in 1974, between 6 and 8% of South Boston High graduates went on to college," whereas the 1979 "class sent 38% of its students to 'post-secondary education,'" and "suspensions (were) down from 1660 in 1974 to 118 (in 1979)." (*Boston Herald*, March 31, 1980, page A6N).

Throughout the mayoral campaign powerful white-controlled media claimed that "growth" explained how Raymond Flynn changed from an "anti-busing," anti-feminist, anti-gay representative of South Boston to a city-wide "populist." People grow because of gradual and dramatic influences in their personal lives that lead them to change. At no point in the campaign did these media explain what personal influences led Flynn to grow from a school boycott organizer in 1974 to a "populist" in 1983 who now claimed to embrace the concerns of all those left out and shut out. Furthermore, the public record reveals that at an interracial clergy-sponsored mayoral debate in November, Flynn himself contradicted his "growth" in recalling the desegregation period: "My record is very clear; again, I'm proud of it. . . . I provided the moral leadership, the political leadership this city needed. I was there, open, dealt with the problem, which was a very difficult problem in 1974." Flynn's actual documented record suggests that this "growth" became a convenient election-year wastebasket into which certain white-owned media could dump contradictions that needed to be explained away.

After the preliminary, the "white-out" of Flynn's record on racial problems, and attempt to minimize racism as a campaign issue were reinforced by *The Boston Globe*. Menzies wrote that no matter whether Flynn or King, who "share much the same philosophies," is elected, "the real winner will be the city of Boston." (Oct. 13, page 21). Nyhan told voters that a "high-minded" campaign means "avoiding the race question" as its injection would polarize the city. (Oct. 16, page A25). A *Globe* editorial declared, "King, Flynn and all their opponents deserve credit for the absence of racial rancor in this election. . . . In the next five weeks, Bostonians hope and expect these high standards to continue." (Oct. 13, page 18). An overriding concern of Germond and Witcover was even set off to highlight their column on "Race and Boston vote": "Can Flynn and King make it through the next four weeks until the Nov. 15 final without straying from the path of racial maturity?" (Oct. 15, page 19). Turner concluded, ". . . if King goes on the attack against Flynn, pointing an accusing finger at the substantial differences in their records, the voters are likely to punish King for it more than Flynn. . . . The voters are not looking for candidates who accentuate divisions." (Oct. 25, page 13). Turner did not specify the "substantial differences in their records" that would "accentuate divisions."

"Real winner?" "High-minded campaign?" "The race question?" "Racial rancor?" "High standards?" "The path of racial maturity?" "Accentuate divisions?" *The Boston Globe* helped to create a climate of "high-mindedness" that condemned as divisive and thus made impossible any real, honest, open, and desperately needed discussion of the two candidates' records on one of Boston's most pervasive problems—which served to protect Flynn's candidacy and hurt King's campaign.

Flynn picked up on the *Globe*'s "high standards," calling King's criticism of his record on racial problems "'confrontation politics,'" which, Flynn said, "'is no longer needed' in Boston." (*The Boston Globe*, Oct. 27, page 1). In a later debate with King, "Flynn proposed that the candidates focus their dialogue for the remainder of the campaign on issues other than race relations. . . . Flynn said the two candidates should not 'let this city take part in any kind of confrontation over race.'" (*The Boston Globe*, Oct. 28, page 22).

In various ways *The Boston Globe* stated that race was not and should not be an issue in the mayoral campaign—while all along reminding the overwhelmingly white electorate over and over again that Mel King was black. *The Globe* constantly referred to him as "the only candidate who is black," "Boston's only black mayoral candidate," "the only black candidate for mayor," "the only black candidate in the race," "the only black in the race," "King: a black ultra liberal independent," "the climate for a black mayoral candidacy is also better today . . ."

Following the primary *The Globe* continued to find a variety of ways of saying it: "King would be the city's first black mayor"; "Boston, for the first time nominated a black"; "he has a good chance of becoming the city's first black chief executive"; "King faces some formidable obstacles in his quest to become the city's first black mayor"; "If you were a black liberal running for mayor in a city where conservative Roman Catholic voters formed the bulk of the electorate, the last thing you'd want is a big stink over suggesting a recently deceased prelate is anti-semitic" (the first sentence of Nyhan's Nov. 6 column called "A costly slip for Mel King"); "the growing willingness of Bostonians to accept a black mayor"; "the first black candidate to become a finalist in a Boston mayoral election."

Globe staff writer Joan Vennochi's extensive profile of Mel King 10 days before the election began with, "The public debate over Melvin H. King as rebel or nonconformist leader began more than 15 years ago. It is still unsettled today as he seeks to become Boston's first black mayor."

Like Vennochi's profile, *Globe* cartoonist Paul Szep's focus on the color of Mel King's skin conveyed a double message to voters. In his "MAYORAL GALLERY," Szep's cartoon poses King as making a V for victory sign with his fingers, and wearing a coat with buttons, worded from left to right, "Boycott," "Down with . . . . . . ," "Black Power," "Elect Mel King," "Save the whales," "BUG," "Boycott Lettuce," and with a peace insignia on the upper left arm of the jacket. (Aug. 28, page A22).

Szep's caricature of King also exploits the very physical features that always have been exaggerated to depict black people in dehumanizing ways. The wide nostrils and thick lips presented to voters an ape-like "King Kong" image, providing subliminal reinforcement for the racist stereotyping of people of color as less than human.

The caricature thus presents a very negative, generalized "Down with . . . . . . ," anti-establishment, sophomoric, dehumanized picture of Mel King, communicating to the white electorate that he is for "Black Power" and therefore by inference against just about everything else, especially their interests. Here the color of Mel King's skin is equated with danger. That danger also is reinforced by the caricature's large, possibly foreboding, threatening, totally black background. The backgrounds of the caricatures of all the other candidates in "SZEP'S MAYORAL GALLERY" are *white*. A picture is worth a thousand words.[3]

Rev. Jesse Jackson has criticized white-owned media for similar attempts to undermine his presidential candidacy. At a news conference on the campus of Virginia Union University, "Mr. Jackson said

What's Black, White and Racist? 155

part of his difficulty (in attracting voters who are white) could be attributed to the fact that he was portrayed in the press as a 'black' candidate, while no such identification was attached to Mr. Mondale and Mr. Hart. He said this pattern was the 'seamy side of racial characterization' that re-inforced racial separation." (*The New York Times*, March 22, 1984, page B8). "Jackson said that it bothered him to be frequently referred to as a black candidate, while Mondale and Hart are never referred to as white candidates. He also said that he is referred to as a black leader, while his opponents are never called white leaders. 'Talking about my skin color is not trying to describe me so much as it is to define me,' he added.... Most whites have 'still not learned that you don't tell a tree by its bark but by the kind of fruit it bears,'" he said. (*The Boston Globe*, March 22, 1984, page 6).

Jackson also stated that his candidacy has been hurt by the media's reinforcement of stereotypes of black people. *The Boston Globe* reported, "Jackson, who has had trouble attracting whites to his *self-styled* [italics added] rainbow coalition, told reporters... 'It's not my fault that whites over their history have developed a disregard for the intelligence of black people.' Reinforcement of stereotypes in the media also has hindered his candidacy, Jackson said, adding that blacks are depicted as 'comic relief, singing, dancing, ballplaying... and generally less intelligent and hard-working.'... White voters, he said, have a 'moral challenge' to overcome historical racial patterns and vote for a black candidate." (*Ibid.*, pages 1 and 6). *The New York Times* reported Jackson as saying, "'It remains a moral challenge, however, to white leadership to make judgments based on character and not based on race.'" (*Ibid.*)

"*Self-styled* rainbow coalition"? *The Boston Globe*'s report of Jackson's criticism of the press contains the very bias Jackson was criticizing. *The Globe* injected its own subtle, unexplained adjective that in itself is designed to confine the "rainbow coalition" to the color of Jesse Jackson's skin.

The Boston Herald "reported": "The Rev. Jesse Jackson, elated at his showing in New York's primary, declared his candidacy and its '*Rainbow Coalition*' *of minority groups* [italics added] a resounding success." (April 4, 1984, page 4). *The Herald* confined the colors of the Rainbow Coalition to "minority groups," thus distorting the identity of a coalition that always has represented white persons and people of color alike.

The aim of influential white-controlled media is to "ghettoize," ignore and, when necessary, depreciate Jackson's presidential candidacy and Rainbow Coalition,[4] as was done to Mel King's candidacy for mayor.

The bias of certain white-owned media's coverage of Boston's mayoral campaign is further seen in their failure to thoroughly research and report their own and other sources of Raymond Flynn's and Mel King's records on Boston's critical racial problems, thus denying the voters this most important comparison between the two candidates. These media also refused to report or analyze the research that had been done which appears in the foregoing.

A week before the October 11 preliminary a group of religious leaders called a press conference to present a statement on why they believed Mel King was the only mayoral candidate qualified to help them bring racial justice and peace to Boston—this issue long recognized by media and citizens alike as foremost in the city. The 9-page statement used *The Boston Globe* and *Boston Herald* as primary sources. It dealt exclusively with Mel King's positive handling of Boston's continuing and severe racial incidents and issues over the years, examples of which have been included in this article. Both print and electronic media were contacted for the press conference. None showed up.

The bias of certain media is also seen in their refusal to report their own public record when it was presented to them.

In a televised mayoral debate, Mel King declared that Flynn's "'inflammatory' statements during the busing crisis" helped to "make Flynn 'unqualified' for the job." (*The Boston Herald,* October 27, page 8). *Boston Herald* reporter Wayne Woodlief called King's headquarters to obtain the specific "inflammatory" statements made by Flynn to which King was referring. The headquarters referred Woodlief to this writer, who was interviewed by Woodlief on October 27. This writer provided examples of Flynn's inflammatory statements and school boycott leader role (which appear in this piece), a 14-page research paper that compared King's and Flynn's record for the last 10 years in response to Boston's extensive racial violence and related issues, and copies of numerous newspaper sources providing the documentation for the research paper, including the *South Boston Tribune* which offered the most thorough publicized account of

Flynn's record, and which, as this writer stressed to Woodlief, was an important source of information about Flynn's public record.

Woodlief also was given newspaper stories on a fire-arms and hand-to-hand combat training program for South Boston youths, which Mayor Kevin H. White and the Boston City Council, in 1979 (when Flynn was a councilor), originally approved for $40,000 in federal funding, until a WGBH-TV investigative report revealed that: the program was for judo and hand-gun courses and not really for recreation and job training; "the 'final training phase' tested the youths on community vigilante proposals"; the project was principally organized by Edward Studley of the South Boston Marshals; and "sentence eleven of the approved application reads, 'Each (of the four project directors) has served on the executive boards of both the South Boston Information Center and the South Boston Marshals....'" (*The Real Paper*, June 2, 1979, pages 5, 15 and 18; *The Boston Globe*, May 19, 1979, pages 13, 14). The intent of this project should have been challenged in the beginning by the City Council and the mayor because of the "vigilanteism" that has driven and kept people of color out of South Boston.

The newspaper clips Woodlief received included a March 13, 1980 *Boston Globe* piece on "250 against busing march in S. Boston," which stated that Edward Studley, a member of the South Boston Marshals, organized the march and that, "Other local personalities who spoke at yesterday's march included such long-time opponents of busing as Boston School Committee member Elvira Pixie Palladino, James Kelly of the South Boston Information Center and City Councilmen Albert O'Neil and Raymond Flynn."

In 1980 also, *Globe* columnist Robert A. Jordan referred to the South Boston Information Center as one of the "racist elements in the city." (August 26, 1980, page 11). In 1979 Headmaster Winegar was quoted as stating that 15 masked white students' vicious stoning of buses carrying black students to South Boston High School occurred four days after "'the South Boston Information Center had an anti-busing rally on the steps of the school.'" (*The Boston Globe*, September 20, 1979, pages 1 and 2). Winegar and legal authorities reportedly believed that adults were behind the stoning and other racial violence in and around South Boston High and other city schools. (*The Boston Herald*, October 24, 1979, page 1, and Sept. 19, 1979, page A3); *The*

Boston Globe, October 23, 1979, page 14). According to *The Real Paper*, James Kelly, president of the South Boston Information Center, who also spoke for the South Boston Marshals as well, has not only been militantly opposed to school desegregation; he pushed "a campaign against the Boston Housing Authority to prevent integrating the South Boston Housing projects"—the campaign included white squatters occupying project apartments to keep people of color our, and Kelly leading a "sit-in outside Mayor (Kevin) White's office demanding an apartment for his latest BHA squatter." (June 2, 1979, pages 15 and 18).

The newspaper stories Woodlief received included the above as well. He also probably knew of Kelly and the South Boston Information Center's adamant opposition to affirmative action in employment to correct the historic discrimination against people of color.

A few days later in a letter this writer asked Woodlief, "How did [City Councilor] Flynn vote on the [gun-training] proposal?" and "What is Flynn's relationship to the South Boston Marshals and to the South Boston Information Center? I don't know."

The perceived racially divisive roles of the South Boston Information Center and South Boston Marshals, and the fact that people of color have been driven and kept from Carson Beach, the streets, dwellings and employment opportunities in South Boston, should have led the media, during this mayoral election especially, to investigate the nature of the two groups' beliefs and activities, what kind of relationship and support, if any, Flynn had with and from them, and where in the public record he dissociated himself from and condemned any activities of their's that were divisive. This important investigative journalism was not performed by Woodlief, nor by others who work for certain white-owned media.

Woodlief said that his article was scheduled to appear in *The Boston Herald* on November 1. When it did not appear, this writer called him, and he said that it would be published on November 6. It did not appear then either. On November 8, *The Boston Herald* endorsed Flynn for mayor. On November 13, two days before the election, a piece by Woodlief appeared called "Flynn anti-busing record: Forceful but non-violent." Woodlief wrote, "Mel King, Flynn's opponent and King supporters claim Flynn made 'inflammatory' remarks, encouraging lawbreaking during the busing crisis. *Flynn has*

What's Black, White and Racist? 159

rebutted that he urged children to stay in school [italics added], and personally sought to keep racial peace. A review of newspaper clippings from that period suggests that Flynn, indeed, was a forceful opponent of court-ordered busing, but he consistently urged his South Boston constituents to resist peacefully, and spoke out against street violence." Woodlief concluded the article with, "*The thrust of Flynn's fight against busing was through the courts* [italics added], and through peaceful pressure on the mayor's office, Congress and the Legislature."

The Boston Herald obtained the inflammatory record detrimental to Flynn's campaign, sat on it, and at the last minute laundered it with the "white-wash" of "red-neck" journalism.

Boston Globe staff also received the research paper on King's and Flynn's records on racial issues, including copies of the extensive newspaper sources for it. Material was hand-delivered on November 1 to staff writer Walter V. Robinson, who was preparing a profile of Flynn for publication. In the letter accompanying the material, this writer called his attention especially to newspaper clippings of the South Boston gun-training proposal in 1979, and asked, "How did Flynn vote on that proposal?" The letter also noted newspaper clips referring to Edward Studley of the South Boston Marshals as organizer of the project, Flynn marching and speaking against "forced busing" with Studley and James Kelly of the South Boston Information Center as late as 1980, and expressed this writer's belief that "the *South Boston Tribune* is a sadly neglected, important source of information on Flynn's ongoing real public record."

Robinson questioned the implication of Flynn's quoted statement, "'I wonder if the Boston media will respond with the same outrage [to the beating of (white) Richard Poleet], as with the beating at City Hall Plaza of [black] Atty. Theodore Landsmark.'" Robinson told this writer that Flynn could have also condemned the beating of Landsmark and the media may not have picked it up. In response this writer delivered to him the *South Boston Tribune* story which reported, "The Boston lawmaker (Flynn) introduced a resolution in the Massachusetts House of Representatives on Tuesday, deploring the senseless beating of (Poleet)...." The vicious beating of Landsmark was not included in Flynn's resolution. This writer said to Robinson, "That should tell you a great deal—as should the other newspaper clips...

especially Flynn and (State Rep.) Flaherty refusing to sign a joint Massachusetts House statement deploring the violence... and then issuing the kind of statement they did."

Robinson's extensive profile on Flynn was published on November 3. He completely ignored all the documentation on Flynn's record this writer had given to him. He told readers that Flynn joined other parents in keeping "his two school-age children home as part of an organized boycott," when in fact *The Boston Globe* reported in 1974 that Flynn was a leader of the boycott. (Sept. 13, 1974, page 3).

Robinson wrote, "Critics of (Flynn's) housing performance often fail to mention Flynn's 1979 rescue of a black youth being pursued by a white gang on Boston Common or his support of human rights and fair housing legislation since he joined the City Council." What Robinson himself failed to mention is that the "white gang" chasing the youth were actually so-called "anti-busing" students demonstrating at the State House—many of them possibly Flynn's own constituents. (*Boston Herald American*, October 20, 1979, pages 1 and A4). The problem he helped to inflame came running in his direction.

Robinson also failed to mention that Flynn and other City Council members rejected a strong "Boston Commission Against Discrimination" proposal in favor of a "Human Rights Commission" with no teeth, because of "a lot of pressure in the Council from racist elements in the city, especially the South Boston Information Center," according to *Globe* columnist Jordan. (August 26, 1980, page 11). And Robinson failed to mention that the only black tenant to move into a South Boston housing project in 1979 under a desegregation plan was forced to leave because of the danger presented by certain of City Councilor Flynn's South Boston neighbors. (*The Boston Globe*, Sept. 8, 1979, page 1).

The day after Robinson's piece *The Globe* published staff writer Joan Vennochi's profile on Mel King. She, too, had received the extensive research paper on King's and Flynn's records. She ignored it. She also ignored King's many and impressive legislative and community achievements, including his initiating in 1979 the "Boston Jobs for Boston People" program which has guaranteed employment for more city residents.

Vennochi chose a "non-conformist" slant for her profile of King, used selective historical events of a controversial nature, quoted particular persons and sources in specific and undocumented ways to

What's Black, White and Racist? 161

support her slant, and colored certain quotes and events with her own subtle interpretations.

She began her profile with, "The public debate over Melvin H. King as rebel or nonconformist leader... is still unsettled today." She then loaded the profile with, "As a protestor in the 60's, King defied the city's business and political establishment..."; "he staged sit-ins... which led to his arrest"; "When the Pope visited Boston in 1979 after the shooting of a black football player in Charlestown, King led a march [it was a walk] to draw attention to the climate of racial disharmony in the city—even though the mayor and the mother of the victim asked him not to"; "some still think of King... chiefly in the role of radical and activist"; "has criticized traditional leadership, black and white"; "his supporters say that King's greatest strength—an unswerving commitment to his own beliefs—can also be viewed as his chief weakness;" "even as a mayoral candidate, King continues to take controversial stands on matters of principle to him, but of seemingly little relevance to the job of being mayor in the view of some political observers"; "his first public controversy involved his firing in 1967 from a job as a South End youth worker"; "it was the public's first view of him practicing the politics of confrontation, and there are still differing perspectives on the stand he took"; "King's role in his next job also became a source of controversy"; "King led the protest that came to symbolize his tenure at the Urban League"; "when King led the Urban League... some newspaper accounts report that he left financial disarray."

Vennochi took Mel King's strength—his unswerving commitment to the beliefs and democratic rights *of all people*—which is the very opposite of "an unswerving commitment to *his own beliefs*"—and suggested that it may really betray a weakness. She left readers with the impression that he could actually be a rigid, rabble-rousing "radical" who uses his principles to flout and offend established authority, and therefore the city may be in for four years of controversy and turmoil if he is elected mayor.

Globe columnist Robert Turner also received the research paper on King's and Flynn's records and documented newspaper clips. Turner had endorsed Mel King before the preliminary. In an accompanying letter, this writer drew his attention to the same concerns expressed to Robinson. Turner did nothing with the documented research on the records of the two candidates.

The Boston Globe stressed throughout the campaign that there was little difference between Mel King and Raymond Flynn. In an October 4 editorial *The Globe* announced that it "is not endorsing a candidate in the Oct. 11 preliminary election for mayor of Boston" because, "In this mayoral election five mayor candidates [who included "Raymond L. Flynn . . . and Melvin H. King"] have demonstrated the experience and intelligence to lead this city capably." On November 8, four days after Vennochi's profile of King and a week before the election, *The Globe* endorsed Flynn for mayor.

Early the morning of November 8 this writer hand-delivered a letter, written the day before, to William O. Taylor, chairman of the Board and Publisher of *The Globe*, with a carbon copy to editor Thomas Winship. Included with the letter were the research paper on King's and Flynn's records on racial issues, the many newspaper clips documenting the research, copies of the correspondence with Robinson and Turner, and this writer's (November 4 published) letter to the editor which was critical of the *Globe*'s coverage of the campaign and which had been rejected as an opposite ed piece (called "Flynn in Like King").

The personal letter to Taylor expressed deep concern about *The Boston Globe*'s coverage of the mayoral campaign, cited Robinson's and Vennochi's profiles as examples, along with Vennochi's profile being followed the next day by two Flynn campaign workers' opposite ed piece the size of two such pieces. The letter concluded, "A commitment to the truth, to the citizens of Boston, to racial justice and peace in our city in the years ahead demands a full and immediate airing of the complete records of Mel King and Raymond Flynn. I urge you to help *The Boston Globe* join in making their records known."

Mr. Taylor replied the same day: "We have been doing our level best to maintain as even a posture as possible in our coverage of the mayoral candidates. Obviously we do better on some days than on others. I think on balance the media have covered the campaign in a positive and generally balanced way."

His letter was followed by a letter (on November 11) from managing editor Matthew V. Storin, who wrote, "Your letter of November 7 to William O. Taylor was referred to me. In an effort to give your material the most dispassionate reading possible, we turned over your letter and accompanying material to Robert Kierstead, our ombudsman. As you know, Mr. Kierstead has not hesitated to publicly criticize *Globe* editorial decisions and policies. In this case he said he found the *Globe*'s coverage of the mayoral campaign to be 'extremely fair.' I myself think that our performance has been exceptionally balanced while recognizing that perfection in this regard is impossible."

The day after the *Globe* and *Boston Herald* endorsed Flynn for mayor, a group of interracial and ecumenical religious leaders called a press conference and presented a documented 7-page statement called "BOSTON MAYORAL CANDIDATE RAYMOND FLYNN'S INCONSISTENCIES AND CAMPAIGN OF DECEPTION: THE RIGHT OF CITIZENS TO KNOW AND OUR RESPONSIBILITY TO INFORM THEM."

The statement stressed that the voters had a right to know all the facts about both candidates, that the press not only had a responsibility to present those facts, but must have faith in the maturity of the voters to make their own decisions, that "it is a commentary on the paternalism of our two daily newspapers of record for having recommended to the voters one candidate as the most qualified to unite our city, without first having shared the full records of both candidates." The statement documented Flynn's deception and contradictions which *The Globe* and *Boston Herald* withheld from the voters. In addition to the statement, the members of the press present also received the documented newspaper clips and the 13-page research paper on Mel King's and Raymond Flynn's records in response to racial violence and related issues.

Reporter Andy Hiller of WBZ-TV4 and a cameraman from WCVB-TV5 covered the press conference, both stations filming the entire statement. They also filmed comments this writer made about *Globe* writers Robinson and Vennochi having the documented research on King's and Flynn's records and ignoring it in their own profiles on the two candidates. Rev. Jonathan Robinson, president of the Greater Boston Interdenominational Ministerial Alliance, consisting of most of the city's black clergy, also expressed his belief that *The Globe* had gone back on its word in endorsing Flynn for mayor in the preliminary because all were qualified.

The press conference was not reported on any WBZ or WCVB television newscast. The evening of Election Day this writer saw Andy Hiller at Mel King's headquarters, and asked him why nothing appeared on WBZ. He said that he called *Globe* publisher William O. Taylor following the press conference, and after talking with Taylor WBZ decided not to report it.

WBZ appears to have allowed Taylor to determine whether the

religious leaders' criticism of Flynn and of *The Boston Globe's* coverage of the mayoral campaign was valid and newsworthy. Hiller actually seemed to be saying that the media is a club, and that truth is dispensable if it conflicts with the self-interests of the members of the club. A well-informed source said that the story circulating around *The Boston Globe* was that the *Globe's* decision to endorse Flynn for mayor was "Taylormade," and created conflict among some staff.

Reporter Sandy Kent and photographer Jim Mahoney of *The Boston Herald* showed up for our press conference. When they discovered Mel King was not present, they called *The Boston Herald* and were told to return rather than stay and cover the conference. *The Boston Herald* had been clearly told that the religious leaders were going to expose Flynn's deception of the public, that they had the documentation to prove it, and that the citizens of Boston had a right to know and they, as religious leaders, had a moral obligation to inform them. At no point was the newspaper told that Mel King would be present. Also attending the press conference and staying to cover it were Ed Weinstock of WHDH, Owen May of WRKO and Daniel Crow of WBCN.

Four days before the election, 40 Roman Catholic Sisters from seven Boston-area congregations released a statement formally endorsing Mel King for mayor, because he had "consistently addressed the unjust systems of our time that prevent people of all races, nationalities and creeds from experiencing the fullness of human life." This powerful endorsement received virtually no attention from *The Boston Globe* and *The Boston Herald*. Whereas, shortly before this endorsement both newspapers devoted considerable negative coverage to Mel King's statement that the late Cardinal Humberto Medeiros of the Boston Archdiocese created an atmosphere for anti-Semitism in issuing a pastoral letter (a week before the 1980 congressional primaries) strongly condemning two pro-choice candidates' sanctioning of abortion, one of whom was U.S. Rep. Barney Frank who is Jewish.

This writer's documented research on Mel King's and Raymond Flynn's records on racial issues was not exhaustive, nor ever presented as such. But it was far more thorough and accurate than what passed for investigative journalism by certain white-controlled media's coverage of their records on what was commonly believed to be the most critical problem facing the city of Boston.

The "printed word" and newscasts at 6 and 11 contain no mystique that sets them apart as mediums of truth. When men and women become editors, columnists, reporters, newscasters, news editors, commentators, and editorial directors, they are not suddenly immune from the white racist status quo in which they were raised and live. They not only report and analyze news, they reflect their own conditioning and the vested interests of those who pay their salaries.

What are the vested interests of those who pay their salaries? Dominant media, banks, insurance companies, corporations and universities have an interlocking relationship: certain of their directors sit on each other's policy-making bodies—and they have determined that *racism is bad for business*. The dominant media, therefore, minimized the city's severe problem of racism as a campaign issue—and hailed Mel King's preliminary win as indicative of racial progress—in an attempt to clean up Boston's racist reputation both nationally and internationally. The mass development of hotels and convention facilities in Boston, the desire to attract young professionals to take up residence in the city's growing number of condominiums and other luxury housing, the attraction of U.S. and foreign students to the metropolitan area's many colleges and universities, and Boston's effort to compete with other U.S. cities as a center for international financial transactions (which includes vying for the business of Third World countries) are all enhanced by convincing people that the racial quality of life in Boston has changed and is progressive.

Mel King presented a serious threat to the racist status quo in Boston. He communicated that threat very clearly in a mayoral debate in saying, "'One major difference between us (he and Flynn): I talk basically and bluntly about discrimination as a serious issue in this city. I don't try to cover it up by saying the problems of South Boston and Roxbury are the same.... If we're talking about the problems of the people of Roxbury, there is racism, and we have to be very clear that there is a difference. And if there's one difference between us, it is that this candidate knows that issue and addresses it very directly and does not hesitate to deal with it. The only way to solve it is to bring it right up front.'" (*The Boston Globe*, Oct. 21, 1983, page 11).

Mel King was a grave threat because he would not do the bidding of the white-controlled structures, to give them—and the city—the appearance of "racial harmony" so that the ingrained racism could continue unchallenged—and not be bad for business. Furthermore, during an overt racial crisis that threatened the racial "social order," he could not be used by white power structures as a spokesperson for the black community merely to urge calm to maintain the "social order." *He was not a white-chosen black leader.*

The leader of Boston's Rainbow Coalition was selected by people of color to represent their interests and right of equal access in white-dominated political, economic, real estate, communications, educational, legal and religious structures in Boston. He also was selected by white persons because he would represent just as vigorously the interests and rights of those victimized by classism, and the integrity of those committed to justice.

King presented a dangerous threat to the status quo not merely because he was black, but also because he truly would represent the interests of *all* the people of Boston. He made it clear that he would change the status quo by using the power of the mayor's office to radically re-organize the city's own employment opportunities, services, treasury, land holdings, legal resources and tax structure to correct historic ingrained discrimination against people of color, and to make sure that white persons as well would not be exploited and oppressed by banks, real estate developers, the business community, universities, the press and other moneyed interests.

Unlike Mel King, Raymond Flynn communicated to the white-controlled power structures that he would maintain and protect their racial status quo. The bottom line of Flynn's campaign was his promise to manage the city in the belief that white and black people face the same problems: *The Boston Globe* reported that, "Flynn, pressed by reporters, repeatedly refused to agree with King's assertion that blacks suffer greater discrimination than do whites. . . . In a later interview, Flynn said several times that both blacks and whites are discriminated against economically, and that he does not believe there are differences between South Boston and Roxbury on racial or economic discrimination issues." (Oct. 21, page 11).

By equating white and black people the same, Flynn reassured the power structures that he would not talk about nor confront the severe *white* racism pervading Boston—which has resulted in far more and far different economic discrimination for people of color than white persons. Flynn gave his word that he would not re-order the city's resources to correct the economic favoritism enjoyed by white persons and economic deprivation endured by people of color precisely because of the color of their skin. In attributing the same kind of economic oppression to white persons as to people of color, Flynn, in effect, communicated to vested and controlling white interests that he would continue the practice of classism's *racism of equality*.[5]

The facts that black and white persons have the same economic needs and that many white persons also are economically oppressed in no way negate racism; these facts are more likely to be used to perpetuate the racism. Flynn's current belief that there are "(no) differences between South Boston and Roxbury on racial or economic discrimination issues" will serve to allow the white controllers of the city's job and housing markets and other resources to continue their exploitative practice of pitting white persons and people of color against each other. Even if Flynn's intentions are good, his perception of economic discrimination accommodates the use of classism to justify racism.

The striking irony in the effort to use classism to undermine the struggle against racism is that the class interests of white workers and special interests of the community of color are both dealt a severe blow. Racism, in the nation's history and in the present, is the most potent weapon to divide working people, to discourage cooperation on issues of pressing mutual concern, and to obscure the nature and identity of the real causes of poverty and injustice. The economic and social consequences of racism affect all races of working people, dragging down wage standards for all, crippling educational opportunities and health services for black and white persons, and damaging the prospects for social change for all races. Thus, a real "classism" requires uncompromising struggle against the special phenomenon of racism. An undifferentiated approach to the problems of poor persons, failing to account for the exceptional character of racism, will only perpetuate division and thus weaken the interests of people of color and white persons alike.

Therefore, as mayor, Raymond Flynn cannot possibly represent the economic interests of people of color if he does not understand or deal with the severe problem of racism in Boston that is the primary cause of their economic discrimination. If he does not confront racism, he will never really help people of color to gain equal access to economic security in the city—regardless of his appointment of certain black persons to positions in his administration, going to a black home which is without heat, having his picture taken with children of color, and his "preachments of racial harmony." (*The Boston Globe* editorial, Nov. 17, 1983).

The status quo uses certain code words to handle—and perpetuate—its racism: "racial harmony," "racial peace," "racial unity"—and "racial tension," "racial unrest," "racial discord." Referring to racism only in terms of surface relationships and symptoms betrays the failure or refusal to recognize and confront the underlying issues of oppression and justice which determine whether there shall be racial harmony or tension. *The Boston Globe* and *The Boston Herald* have continually reduced the city's severe problem of racism to "racial harmony" and "racial tension."

Boston Globe editorials will tell Mayor Raymond Flynn when overt racial violence erupts—just as they told Mayor Kevin White periodically for 16 years before—the cause of Boston's racial problems and what he should do about it. Mel King would tell *The Boston Globe* that it is part of the problem and what *The Globe* should do about it.

Raymond Flynn would pick up a snow shovel in Copley Square and pose for a *Boston Herald* photographer to take his picture shoveling snow from a sidewalk painting of Dr. Martin Luther King, Jr. (January 14, 1984, page 6). Mel King would pose the tragic implication of Dr. King's dream: that contrary to Flynn's belief, children of color in Roxbury, unlike white children in South Boston, are being judged by the color of their skin and not by the content of their character.

Certain readers may argue that the article's criticism of Raymond Flynn is unfair because he should be given a chance to prove himself as mayor. This argument fails to comprehend that the focus of the article is on the media's role in Flynn's election and the moral and political implications of their role. *The issue herein is not giving Raymond Flynn a chance but how he got his chance.*

Flynn's record on racial issues in Boston is important for more than the way it was used—or misused—in getting him elected. It is also important for those who care about the present and future political health, viability and unity of the city. Disclosure of that record must not imply that his views and policies are unalterable. Our expectations about elected officials, however, and the demands that we make upon them are inevitably shaped and influenced by their records. The record reveals that pressure—and lots of it—is essential to propel Mayor Raymond Flynn toward growth, depth and commitment, if he is to help lead this city to equal access and justice—and thus to racial unity. An accurate disclosure of the record, therefore, is not a negative and static judgement. Quite the contrary, it is a dynamic and constructive tool to alert the community and to foster change.

The *Boston Globe* told us in various ways that King and Flynn were similar, that the "high-minded" approach of all the candidates made the "preliminary a healing and cathartic experience," that "the campaign took Boston beyond the race question" (David Nyhan's column of October 6, 1983 page A25): that "compounding Mel King's problem is that both he and Flynn share much the same philosophies," that "both claim to be healers and can prove it." (Ian Menzies column of October 13, 1983 page 21).

If, as *The Globe* stressed, King and Flynn "share much the same philosophies," Flynn's "populism" became especially popular with moneyed people after the preliminary. Following the election it was reported that over half of the $863,082 contributed to his campaign was received after the October 11 preliminary. (*The Boston Globe*, January 11, 1984, page 13). The total contributed was far more than twice King's reported total of $379,068. Flynn also received 68 individual contributions of $1,000, whereas King received only 17 such contributions. (*Ibid.*; *The Boston Globe*, January 14, 1984 page 5).

The Globe and certain other white-controlled media and leaders' reporting of how similar King and Flynn were, how "healing and cathartic" the preliminary was for Boston, and how injecting "the race question" into the campaign would polarize the city while constantly reminding voters that Mel King was "the only black candidate for mayor" *helped to prepare Boston's overwhelmingly white electorate (80%) to vote along racial lines.* Flynn received around 85% of the white electorate vote. (*The Bay State Banner*, November 24, 1983, page 1; *The Boston Globe*, November 17, page 29). The deciding factor in the election was the color of the candidates' skin.

Mel King's victory in the preliminary was interpreted by certain white-controlled media as indicating that Boston has progressed racially. The day after the preliminary *Globe* columnist Turner's front-page "News Analysis" called "A changing city votes to take new direction in its leadership" began with, "Boston voters yesterday took a bold step down a path the city has never traveled before. The city that was ripped by racial division just 10 years ago dramatically thrust off that memory, nominating Melvin H. King, the first black man in Boston history to achieve that position."

Globe associate editor Menzies, in a column called "Boston's the real winner," assumed, "Obviously, it won't be easy for media visitors to forget Boston's long, strife-torn racist history; nor should they. But something happened in this, one of the oldest of American cities, that is truly momentous. We are seeing for the first time a growth of the spirit, instead of just buildings; a humanitarian concern for people above and beyond steel, concrete and glass. It is a cry for humanitarian balance and racial peace. . . . A King win in Boston would be a real upset but . . . no matter what happens the real winner will be the city of Boston." (Oct. 13, 1983, page 21).

Columnist Nyhan declared, "Boston's mayoral campaign was remarkable for a city that had come to symbolize racist hatred in the streets. The [preliminary] campaign was free of race-baiting, racial incidents and the kind of rhetoric that made the city ashamed in the recent past. . . . Thanks to a largely issue-oriented campaign, and the high-minded approach taken by all the major candidates in the field, the Boston preliminary was a healing and cathartic experience. The campaign took Boston beyond the race question: the victors won on plain concerns of working class voters." (Oct. 16, 1983, page A25).

The Globe's editorial after the preliminary stated, "Much of the national and international commentary about Tuesday's preliminary election here will focus on King's strong support city-wide as a black candidate in a city wracked a decade ago by racial violence. King, Flynn and all their opponents deserve credit for the absence of racial rancor in this election. In the next five weeks, Bostonians hope and expect those high standards to continue."

The day after the preliminary *The Boston Herald*'s editorial, called "Boston's big win," asserted, "The victory of King . . . says a good deal about how far Boston has come in the past decade, how much Boston has grown up. No matter what November brings, King's supporters will at least have proven that it is quality, qualifications, energy and drive that count. No, the politics of race and bigotry have not been banished from this city, we are sad to say, but they have been dealt a serious blow. All of the candidates in this race have made it clear that racial bigotry is not acceptable, is not respectable, and we can all be proud of that."

The Globe editorial endorsing Flynn, called "Flynn for mayor," commented, "King's success in the preliminary election, the growing willingness of Bostonians to accept a black mayor and the striking increase in political participation by blacks and Latinos are Mel King's lasting contributions." (Nov. 8, 1983).

The November 17 *Globe* editorial wrapped up the election: "Ray Flynn told his cheering supporters at the Park Plaza that 'tonight Boston made history' by hearing the voice of all its neighborhoods. After his long mayoral campaign, that assertion is true.... The headquarters of losing candidates are generally as cheerful as tombs.... It was different Tuesday night at the Sheraton Boston because Mel King gave his followers and all Bostonians some truths to celebrate.... King's eloquence and dignity helped Boston take 'the giant step forward' that he said the mayoral campaign represented. A white candidate beat a black candidate 2 to 1, so in media shorthand... Boston's reputation as 'racially troubled' remains all too secure. Yet, Tuesdays election showed one important demographic fact in this year of the black vote: proportionately, more white Bostonians voted for Mel King than white Chicagoans voted for Mayor Harold Washington.... As he so often has in the past, Mel King stated the agenda clearly: 'The task before Mayor-elect Flynn is to foster an understanding in Boston which will eradicate the pervasive and disruptive aspects of racism, that will mandate formal recognition of comparable pay and economic equality for women in this city and will make real those goals of Boston as an open and accessible city and that will result in sound, compassionate and responsible fiscal management—and we all must help.'"

With Mel King's victory in the preliminary and defeat in the election, the racist status quo now has it both ways. Its perpetuators, apologists and chaplains can point to King's preliminary win as indicating that Boston has progressed racially in the knowledge that business as usual will continue. The heralding of King's preliminary win as racial progress is *the big lie!*—a "consolation prize" designed to cover up and to pacify.

A classic example of what's black and white and racist all over is *Globe* columnist Nyhan's assessment of the election: "All told, it was a marvelous year for Boston. Racism was beaten back, but not eradicated.... Free of cheap shots, it was the most gentlemanly mayoral race in the city's recent history, a credit to the finalists and those they left behind in the preliminary. It wasn't there for King. But it will be there some year soon for another black, maybe one whose mother is a cleaning lady [like Flynn's mother who was a "cleaning lady" as Nyhan wrote at the beginning of his column]. It can happen." (*The Boston Globe,* Nov. 17, 1983, page 29).

What happened was that the mayoral campaign and election are a "prophetic" example of Orwell's 1984. If Orwell had been black—or liberated from his own racist society—he would have known in 1948 that "1984" already existed for people of color. Mel King could put on a tie and suit and wear a smile, but he could not change the color of his skin.

Contrary to certain white-controlled media's big lie and to their accommodating new mayor's understanding of "economic discrimination" as affecting white persons and people of color equally, the bottom line of the election is that in 1984 a white man from South Boston can become mayor of Boston and a black man from the South End cannot. That is the reality which must continue to be understood and confronted if the next mayor—or president—is to be elected because of his character and not the color of his skin—or her skin or sex. In the case of Boston's 1983 mayoral election, there is nothing more informative than "yesterday's newspaper."

Notes

1. Shortly after endorsing Flynn, Rev. Kelley told this writer that the people of South Boston would not accept Mel King as mayor, and that he feared they would act out violently in the streets against black people if he were elected—even to the point that King himself might be assassinated. The candidate he reportedly said could " 'bring this city together' " was the state rep. for nine years of the very people whom he feared would tear it apart if Mel King were elected mayor. It also is to be stated that Rev. Kelley's church is not the largest black congregation in Boston. Moreover, many in the congregation did not support Rev. Kelley. Mel King was invited to speak, and given a standing ovation.

2. Mel King was a political leader and had spoken out consistently. Was Winegar revealing an inability to recognize the leadership of a politician who was black? Why did he not also comment during the mayoral campaign about Mel King's role in helping to achieve school desegregation and quality education? Why did not the media solicit and report Winegar's views about King's role?

3. "SZEP'S PRESIDENTIAL GALLERY" contains a similarly depreciating caricature of Rev. Jesse Jackson. He pictures Jackson wearing a clerical robe, with emblems of a cross on both sides of a stole also draped over his shoulders, holding an open book in his hands, from which he is reading with a sanctimoniously opened mouth, the book marked with a cross on the bridge and another cross on the front cover underneath the title of the book, "*Jesse Saves.*" (Feb. 26, 1984, page 64). When Jackson announced his candidacy, Szep's cartoon, called "Jesse Jackson considering run for presidency," had Jackson holding a mirror up, looking into it with a self-admiring facial expression and saying, ".... One small step for blacks... one giant leap for Jesse Jackson." In our white racist society, people of color are allowed only "one small step" of progress. Thus the attempt to depreciate a black man who dares to think that he is worthy of living in the "White House."

4. After Jackson's successful effort to secure the release of Lt. Robert Goodman from Syria, his candidacy began to receive a favorable public response. Three weeks before the New Hampshire primary a Gallup Poll showed Jackson edging into second place among prospective Democratic primary voters. He also registered a strong 16% in a New Hampshire pre-primary poll. At that point *The New York Times* began a series of front-page stories on financial contributions by the Arab League to Jackson's PUSH organization. Soon thereafter reports began to circulate in the press about a 19-page "confidential" document prepared by the Anti-Defamation League which alleged that Jackson had on various occasions uttered anti-Semitic remarks. Jackson's reference to Jewish people as "Hymies" and to New York City as "Hymietown," uttered in an off-hand, off the record fashion, was catapulted into a national cause celebre. On the other hand, Jackson's self-criticism apology for the remarks and his call for dialogue between the black and Jewish communities in an appearance at a New Hampshire synagogue was either reported summarily or totally ignored by the media. Similarly, when Jackson appeared before B'nai Brith in Massachusetts, the media ignored his careful and richly textured address, in which he called for a "triologue" between Jewish, black and Arab people to promote reconciliation and peace. The media concentrated instead upon a handful of anti-Jackson demonstrators and upon a series of hectoring, hostile questions from a panel. The aim of this treatment by the media was to undermine the moral authority and widespread appeal of the Rainbow Coalition and to hinder efforts to broaden its political base. As the presidential campaign continued to unfold, Jackson was characterized repeatedly as the candidate of a narrow constituency. His personality was manipulated to stress alleged flaws; a double standard was applied wherein people of color were again placed in the position of being asked to support candidates who are white whose views on racial matters were by no means totally acceptable, while support for Jackson was predicated upon a demand for perfection in the eyes of voters who are white.

5. Racism herein means white racism. To qualify for racist behavior, a group has to have political, economic and legal power to oppress another group. People of color do not have that power.

This understanding of racism means that white people who are physically assaulted by black persons are actually victims of *white* racism—of the racism ingrained in our political, economic, legal, educational and other structures that favors them. The overt violence of people of color toward white persons is not racist but a reaction to their own historic and continuing systemic oppression. This fact does not lessen the tragedy for white victims of white racism nor the culpability of black people who choose physically violent ways to deal with their own far more violent and insidious institutionalized oppression. But this fact does reveal that the real perpetuators of the problem include those who engage in the racism of equality by sweeping embedded institutional racism under the rug of 'equality' in the face of economic problems—or when related overt racial violence threatens the racial hierarchy's "social order."

Mayor Flynn is to be commended for his visibility in going to the scene of individual physical acts of racial violence and speaking out against them. But his present belief that white persons and people of color face the same economic discrimination suggests that he may be prone to engage in the racism of equality in dealing with overt racial violence, and not only in handling economic issues. His position could be that racial violence consists of overt individual acts of physical violence between white and black persons (*youths especially*), and that black and white persons therefore are equally guilty of racial violence. This position prevails in Boston, and serves to divert attention from the underlying white economic/political/legal hierarchy—that oppresses white persons as well as people of color.

The racism of equality is a form of "white magic" used by Boston media especially to interpret overt racial violence and related economic oppression. (See "The 'White Magic' of Systemic Racism," by this writer, *The Crisis*, official organ of the NAACP, Nov. 1978). The racism of equality is also commonly practiced by mainstream religious leaders when forced to deal with overt violence threatening the racial hierarchy's "social order." (See "Religion and White Racism in Boston," by this writer, published in a special issue on "Racial Relations in Boston: The Problem and Its Resolution," *Debate and Understanding*, Journal of Boston University's Martin Luther King, Jr., Center, Summer of 1983).

The realization by white people that they are actually victims of white racism—both as objects of violence and economically—can help them to understand and direct their courage and influence toward the deeper causes of their own victimization. In addition, they can refuse to be manipulated in the face of economic problems by those who stress equality of need between them and people of color in an attempt to keep both groups quiet, to pit them against each other, to prevent them from joining forces to confront common economic oppression created by white economic hierarchy.

VIII

Black Politics In America: From Access to Power

James Jennings

There is a new black politics emerging powerfully in urban America. Black politics today is already becoming substantially different from black politics of a few years ago. In recent years the number of blacks participating in electoral politics has increased rapidly. The joint Center for Political Studies in Washington, D.C. has reported, for example, that 600,000 blacks registered between 1980 and 1982; and the number of black elected officials nationwide rose by 8.6% between July 1982 and July 1983. In this context of increasing black political participation, a new kind of electoral politics is unfolding in black communities.

There are many examples of black electoral activism substantially different from that of just a few years ago. The election of Eddie James Carthan in Tchula, Mississippi, Barbara Mouton in East Palo Alto, California, Harold Washington in Chicago, and Gus Newport in Berkeley, California, illustrate a politics quite unlike what has been usual in post-World War II American cities. The black and Latino vote for New York City mayoral candidate Frank Barbaro in 1981 should also be viewed as distinct from recent minority political behavior in that major city. The mayoral candidacy of Mel King in Boston in 1979 and 1983, and William Murphy in Baltimore in 1983, as well as the budding organizations of progressive black political independents like elected officials Al Vann and Roger Green in Brooklyn, are additional examples.

On a national level, the electoral efforts of Rev. Jesse Jackson also represented the emergence of a new kind of black politics. Largely because of these developments, when one discusses urban politics today, it is necessary to describe two "faces" of politics, each representing different sets of issues, actors, orientation, and style.

One "face" of local politics is quite traditional. It basically seeks to maintain the arrangement of power that has characterized major American cities since World War II. Initially, the important actors in American local politics were private interest groups, the federal government, and mayors and their machines. In the late 1950s, the public service unions were added to this urban "executive coalition."[1] During the 1960s, the black thrust for political participation culminated in the community control movement, and the call for Black Power in American cities. Although the post-World War II urban executive coalition acceded some concessions to blacks and other citizens' groups inspired by the black community, an institutionalization of membership into the ruling partnership was never offered. Local government did not invite blacks, or the poor, to join the partnerships of the powerful; instead, temporary political arrangements and reforms were offered. Many of these reforms have not resulted in the replacement or qualitative change of the urban executive coalition.

Political participation may be directed either at structural change in the distribution of wealth and power, or at the maintenance of the status quo. The latter is characterized by limited flexibility (liberalism) or resistance (conservatism), but what is emphasized is continuity in social relations and political stability. The emerging progressive face of electoral politics focuses on the well-being of people, regardless of its effect on the urban executive coalition's political stability. Specific electoral activities under the two faces of urban politics may be similar in some cases; both, for example, call for mass political participation, the utilization of the franchise as a means of holding government accountable, and the mobilization of voter support for candidates of choice. But while the thrust of traditional electoral activism is to secure benefits from those holding wealth and power in this country, the alternative is to dislodge the holders and controllers of wealth; it is to force a more equitable distribution of the wealth created by the people of America. It is this very position that allows the progressive face of politics to raise local issues within national and international contexts. This is seldom done under the old face of local politics. Under the progressive face of local politics, activists understand the fiscal links between the militarization of American society and the quality of life in the city. Under a progressive orientation, nuclear proliferation, business investments in South Africa, military adventurism in Central America are, in fact, local issues.

Traditional electoral politics essentially is a "buffer" process. It keeps the populace, the poor, the working class—and blacks especially—from effectively confronting "private" decision-makers.[2] Traditional electoral activism seeks to manage this natural conflict in a way that renders it innocuous to interests that control wealth and power; leadership operating under this framework perceives itself as controlling, rather than representing, those on the bottom of America's socioeconomic ladder. This leadership uses minor or non-systematic patronage inducements to satisfy the wants of the populace at various levels of society.[3] Traditional electoral leadership behaves as broker between powerful partners of the urban executive coalition and the citizenry.[4]

The questions placed upon a city's public agenda within the confines of traditional local politics are well known and repetitive throughout urban America: How can we attract big business for "downtown" economic development? How can we build more office spaces and highrise luxury hotels? In effect, how can we make life easier for those who don't live in the city, but control the city? Which human and social services can be reduced in order to relieve the partners of the executive coalition of fiscal pressures? How can the public schools become more responsive to the needs of the business community? These are the important questions under the old face of local politics. But under the progressive face of electoral politics, new questions must be raised. Martin Luther King, Jr., in what could easily be one of the most important contributions to the study of urban politics, *Where do We Go From Here: Chaos or Community?*, offers a framework by which to ask questions about the direction of local politics:

> The stability of the large world house which is ours will involve a revolution of values to accompany the scientific and freedom revolutions engulfing the earth. We must rapidly begin to shift from a "thing"-oriented society to a "person"-oriented society. When machines and computers, profit motives and property rights are considered more important than people, the giant triplets of racism, materialism and militarism are incapable of being conquered. A civilization can flounder as readily in the face of moral and spiritual bankruptcy as it can through financial bankruptcy.[5]

Martin Luther King, Jr.'s analysis provides progressive activists with an overall conceptual framework by which to select, define, and prioritize the social and economic issues facing urban America.

The ruling urban executive coalition of American cities reflects the "old" face of local politics. Within this context, the problems of the city are approached in ways that do not threaten or interrupt the distribution or flow of power, money, status, and privilege. Local politics currently operates within a managerial or "technocratic" framework; here, the specific distribution of power and wealth is not questioned. This managerial approach to local politics dictates the substance and the style of electoral campaigns. For example, electoral challengers to incumbents usually present themselves as better managers or technicians; under the old face of local politics, seekers of electoral office do not offer themselves as leaders of the citizenry, but as effective brokers. And, as such, the major function of mayors elected within this context is to mediate the needs of various citizens' groups with the wealth and power *status quo*. In other words, the basic problem faced by these managers is how to accommodate the social and economic problems facing blacks, the poor, and the working class, within the present hierarchy of wealth and power.

The "old" face of politics has failed to meet the needs of ordinary citizens; this is most evident when we look at black communities in urban America. Indeed, a depressed socioeconomic status has consistently characterized black city life for generations; and today, conditions are worsening. Because of the absence of a commitment to eradicate poverty and racism, and shifting political winds confined to a conservative-liberal continuum, we find that blacks and the poor are losing even the token gains made in the 1960s.

RACE AND THE DEMOCRATIC PARTY

While sensing that something different was emerging in the black community at the local and national levels, Walter Mondale and most of the leadership of the Democratic Party misread or misunderstood not only the intensity of black political sentiment but also the significance of it for the party, and indeed, for American society.

The debacle of Walter Mondale on November 6, 1984, illustrated the ineffective approach of the Democratic Party in maintaining the loyalty of traditionally white Democratic voters. At the same time, the Democratic Party and its intelligentsia have failed to acknowledge that one of the junior partners of the previously successful New Deal coalition has become dissatisfied. The black community is now opting to exercise participation and leadership in a way unprecedented in national party politics.

In a Gallup Poll conducted in the summer before the election, it was found that 87.1% of southern blacks disapproved of Reagan's economic policies, and almost half of all blacks felt that they are worse off under Reagan than they were under Carter.

In the Summer of 1984, the Joint Center for Political Studies commissioned a Gallup Poll which found that 72% of all blacks surveyed considered President Reagan "prejudiced."[6] Manning Marable has written that "the ideological glue of Reaganism was racism."[7] Race *was* a factor in this election, but this does not necessarily distinguish the 1984 presidential election from earlier ones. White voters did support Reagan, in part, for his stance on racial issues. Southern whites who supported the president, for example, opposed affirmative action, 77% to 5%; they supported the Administration's Civil Rights policies by 52% to 26%. The racial messages were emphasized with sublimal suggestions that "troublesome" blacks dissatisfied with America could be categorized with unfriendly foreign elements. This suggestion was made continually in the way the media covered the presidential campaign. For instance, this was illustrated pointedly when journalist Marvin Kalb asked Jesse Jackson on "Face the Nation," the weekly news program: ". . . Do you consider yourself an American or a black?"

Due to the growing demographic and political influence of blacks in major American cities, the Democratic Party can only remain competitive at the national level if it restructures itself in ways which increase its accessibility to black political activists. The Democratic Party has reached a historic "Catch 22" situation. Tom Wicker of *The New York Times* has described it as an "identity crisis for the Democrats."[8] A similar crisis faced the Democratic Party in 1964. But the party leadership was able to resolve the earlier crisis by offering blacks a semblance of access. This kind of incomplete solution is no longer possible. Blacks are no longer interested in the "junior partner" status reserved for them by the traditional power brokers in America. Blacks are now demanding not only an equitable level of access, but also answers to fundamental issues regarding the use and distribution of wealth and power. This does present a quandary to some sectors of American politics. If American liberal leadership acknowledges the heightened political significance of the black community, and dares to respond to it, many white voters will continue to abandon the ranks of the Democrats, and become cannon fodder for the Republican Party. Although this political puzzle has been identified by party activists and pundits, as yet the problem has not been resolved by the Democratic Party.

The strength of the Democratic Party in various periods after the New Deal was due in part to its appeal and control of the "center" in the American political spectrum. Today, this sector is withering away. The Democratic Party maintained majority status in most national elections so long as blacks remained loyal to the party. But, as blacks begin to demand a bigger share of power within the party, white voters will become increasingly threatened. Democrats now find themselves in this political predicament because the problem of racism has never been dealt with in a manner that challenges the hierarchy of power and wealth itself in American society. The Democratic Party has planted and nurtured the seeds of its own demise, because it did not issue this challenge; it did not confront the foundations of racism in this society during the 1940s, 1950s and 1960s.

The Democratic Party has reached a point in its history where it can no longer ignore black voters. But to remain competitive with the Republican Party, it cannot alienate its declining number of white voters. In 1984, this quagmire was resolved temporarily (and only partially) by denying blacks the level of access which their loyalty and activism demanded, but making promises for the future. Jesse Jackson received 18% of the overall primary vote, but he received only 10% of the delegates at the national party convention. Walter Mondale, meanwhile, received 39% of the primary vote, but half (49%) of the delegates. According to black activists, this kind of political imbalance cannot continue. The black community has grown not only in numbers but also in political sophistication. It will be increasingly difficult to dampen the potential electoral influence of blacks by denying them access to party structures and processes.

The year 1964 cannot be repeated for the Democratic Party. Blacks permitted the Democratic Party to devise a solution to this problem in 1964 in such a way that allowed the party to avoid confronting the problem posed here. The demands presented by the Mississippi

Freedom Democratic Party forewarned the Democratic Party that eventually, the problem of racism in America must be confronted. The Democratic Party has had twenty years to respond to this challenge. Today, the Democratic Party will either alienate black voters or white voters at the national level. The outcome of the Democratic Party's "Fairness Commission" to review the 1988 delegate selection process could very well be a major factor in determining whether or not blacks remain in the party.

Although massive black support for the Democratic Party's presidential nominee was not enough to defeat President Reagan, blacks who voted were influential in several Senate and House races in 1984. The black vote was instrumental in the defeat of Republican incumbent Charles Percy of Illinois. This vote also allowed U.S. Senatorial incumbents Howell Heflin of Alabama and Carl Levin of Michigan to defeat Republican opponents who carried the majority of white voters in these states. Several candidates won Congressional seats due to black voter support. These include Steve Neal and Brit Hefner of North Carolina, Ben Erdreich of Alabama, Wayne Dowdy of Mississippi, Robin Tallon of South Carolina, Bruce Morrison of Connecticut and Jim Jones of Oklahoma. The black vote will remain influential, especially in close elections, due to its growing size and concentration in large central cities and pivotal states. Because blacks are voting in greater numbers as a bloc, this fact will also ensure their continuing influential role in American elections. The realization of this strength is emerging powerfully at the same time that demographic developments portend continued significant and rapid growth of the black urban population. It is clear that at least in the electoral arena, black votes could represent a force for major social change in this society.

The black community of America and its leadership must begin to answer political questions which carry major societal implications. Black activists must now analyze their current and future roles in American politics at the local and national levels. The influence of black voters in local and national arenas has been firmly established. Their political decisions will have a great impact on the future of American society. But the growing numbers of black voters may not be the major reason for this; a more important reason may be that blacks, as a major social grouping in this society, represent a constant potential threat to political and economic stability. As social analyst

James Boggs argued a few years ago: "... even though black Americans are a minority in the U.S., they represent (a great) threat to the American system... Because once the bottom of a system begins to explode, then the whole system is threatened."[9] Even in the electoral arena, blacks have the potential to disrupt America politically and economically. As the theoretical possibilities of electorally-based community action win new adherents in the black community, the tendency to challenge the economic status quo will increase; this is because, in toto, the economic and cultural interests of blacks in this country are in a state of structural contradiction with the economic and political status quo.

Growing black political activism at this time in America reflects a radicalization of the black community. This means that greater numbers of blacks are willing to support public policies which challenge the traditional values and norms of American politics.

The activists who are emerging as the spokespersons for renewed activism in the black community are not confined to the usual conceptual boundaries of local politics as described by political scientist Robert Dahl in his classic work, *Who Governs*.[10] Black activists are raising new issues, offering creative ways of responding to pressing social problems, and are not defensive about challenging aggressively American values and economic practices protective of wealth and the kinds of social relationships which flow from wealth.

Generally, blacks occupy a "left" position on the American political spectrum. Some soft evidence for this is reflected in the numerous opinion polls comparing black and white political and social attitudes in this country. At a much higher level than whites, blacks can be supportive of public policy frameworks which challenge, in effect, the way wealth is accumulated and distributed in American society. It is significant that sectors in the black community most supportive of actions and strategies which might be described as "radical" have not (in more recent periods) participated extensively in the electoral arena. But these are the sectors which are now beginning to play a more prominent role in the electoral arenas of black America.

This new political surge is being led and supported by blacks who have heretofore rejected electoral activism as a tool for substantive change in the black community. Many who are now participating in progressive electoral campaigns rejected electoral participation just a few years ago. Black intellectuals and activists on the left, as well as the black underclass, never fully accepted the use of electoral politics for meaningful change. Electoral politics were dominated by individuals and groups that sought accommodation to the power status quo. But the most that was ever available within the *status quo* was periodic patronage for a few gatekeepers in the black community. Traditional politics cannot respond effectively to the social and economic needs of youth, the poor, or the working-class sectors of black America. Progressive electoral activism offers a welcome mat to blacks who have found very little use for traditional electoral activism.

The crucial role of black political leadership in the development of progressive politics at the local level is a logical extension of the socioeconomic status of black urban life. In other words, it is based on the fact that "... blacks are at the center of basic conflicts in most Northern cities... They constitute the racial group whose interests and activities have been most antagonistic to established institutions and better-off strata."[11] It is the black community that has the most to gain from raising fundamental questions about the values and assumptions that underlie our society. Blacks will be in the forefront of this because the contradictions between these values and socioeconomic realities are most evident in black communities. The development of the progressive face of politics in urban America signals the emergence of black political leadership as a major force in our society. This leadership has been thrust upon blacks by American history. The strength and vitality of the new face of urban politics will come from the black community—quite a different role from the one reserved for blacks under the old face of urban politics.

It is because the black community is experiencing a process of radicalization that the major political issue for blacks in America is no longer mere access. No longer are blacks seeking only inclusion in the pluralist processes of this society. The resolution of oppressive life conditions for blacks requires approaches which will incorporate ways of redistributing wealth in America. For those who listened, this was part of the message presented in the Jesse Jackson platform. But this part of the message was rejected by the leadership of the Democratic Party.

As the political influence of the black community grows, activists must consider various strategic queries. If the Democratic Party continues to resist demands for greater black inclusion, at what point does black leadership begin to build coalitions or parties independent of the Democratic Party? In which particular electoral arenas can this be done? While these questions must be addressed by black political activists around the country, other related questions arise in specific American cities. In Tchula, Mississippi, for example, the political and physical repression directed against leftist electoral activists was a clear, violent message of discouragement for the black citizenry.[12] In this small town, private business interests apparently were threatened by the kind of public agenda pursued by black Mayor Eddie James Carthan. In a town like Tchula, the black community cannot rely on the Democratic Party to represent its interests. Private sector actors in Mississippi simply would not allow the citizens of Tchula the political practice to make public decisions contrary to the interests of those controlling social and economic power. While the politics reflected in Eddie James Carthan's mayoral campaign and brief administration are similar in orientation, substance and style to the campaign of Mel King in Boston, the two black communities have different "structural" positions. Blacks in Boston, although not yet representative of a majority of the city's population, *are* in a position of greater potential influence in the local economy and polity than are the blacks in Tchula.

Black activists interested in the development of a progressive agenda in a city like Chicago have yet a different set of tactical and logistical problems. Unlike Boston, the campaign of a progressive black mayoral candidate was successful. Here, black activists are immediately faced with a major tactical question: how to maintain the momentum generated among blacks and Latinos around the Harold Washington campaign. The level of political participation in the black community was unusually intense. Can this recur in four years? Assuming that blacks, Latinos and approximately 15% of the city's white voters who consider themselves liberal or progressive continue to support Mayor Washington, it is possible that the next mayoral election will be a two-person race: Mayor Washington could be pitted against someone like City Alderman Edward Vydrlyak or another individual representing the majority of whites in Chicago. It is safe to say, even now, that if Washington is perceived as a strong contender, his opponent could seek to develop a white backlash in order to counter the political fervor reflected among blacks in Washington's first successful mayoral campaign.

One sure way of counterbalancing this new black political sentiment is to remind whites of the consequences inherent in higher levels of black political participation. This reminder will get a substantial number of whites to register and turn out in elections. This, in fact, was part of the Republican Party's national strategy for victory in the South. As Jesse Jackson helped to register thousands of new black voters, conservative whites scrambled to register in order to counter the growing influence of newly-registered blacks. According to the Committee for the Study of the American Electorate, 173 trade associations and 88 corporations raised between 8 to 22 million dollars for the Republican Party to register white, suburban and conservative voters in the West and South. Obviously, this strategy worked in many parts of the country.

As described above, the Jackson campaign reflected a crystallization of efforts by the black electorate to call for equality. There are at least two new developments which help to differentiate the current movement from earlier periods of black protest. One is the growing realization among many sectors in the black community that for them to gain full equality, a lopsided and inequitable distribution of wealth in American society must be challenged; secondly, there is a reawakening of political nationalism in the black community. This is generating a broad base politics of systemic interests, rather than a politics based on personalities or patronage.

One of the most momentous developments of Jesse Jackson's presidential campaign was the support extended him by Minister Louis Farrakhan, leader of the Nation of Islam, or the "Black Muslims." Many long time black activists immediately realized the importance of this alliance. This event represented the confluence of the legacies of Malcolm X and Martin Luther King, Jr. These two individuals were probably the most politically prominent individuals in the black community after World War II. Though these two are cast in different lights by some, they reflected the same growing mood of anger and alienation in black America.

In 1984, a disciple of Martin Luther King, Jr. and another black leader representing the lineage of Malcolm X finally united to share their visions. This was a significant and foreboding event for the future of American politics; it suggested that there *is* a strong and politically vibrant nationalistic sentiment among blacks in this country. Due to the increasing impoverishment of blacks, this nationalistic sentiment could possibly become the foundation of a massive social and political movement erupting powerfully in major American cities.

The Jackson campaign, the Washington victory, the King mayoral campaigns in Boston, and other electoral struggles reflect a continuity with earlier protest periods. But these recent electoral contests also portend major struggles to alter American society, socially and economically. An indication of this may be the kinds of public policies and issues being raised by black political activists today. Many of these issues have not previously been presented to the American citizenry as 'local politics.' Structures and processes associated with local elections usually do not support the discussion of "key" issues which challenge the way in which power in a local arena is distributed.[13] Public policy can be approached in a way which does not question the conceptual boundaries established by traditional rules of the political game. But public policy can also be approached, at least theoretically, in ways which do not accept as given the various institutional relationships and values which generally have been established and supported in the electoral arenas of major American cities.

FROM ACCESS TO POWER

Traditional local politics seem to generate the most intergroup conflict and tensions around issues of "access." While access issues are prominent in American local politics, they do not necessarily question the usefulness or even the legitimacy of established public structures for the resolution of various social and economic problems. Access issues, however, have generated great levels of stress among political actors, precisely because these kinds of issues could eventually lead to challenges to the existing organization and distribution of wealth and power. For example, affirmative action as an issue of access does not necessarily threaten the institutional relationships or organizational values which have been supported by major political actors in urban America. As a matter of fact, affirmative action could very well represent an important resource for the reform and therefore, a strengthening of established institutional relationships in the large city. Leaders of the business and civic communities whose personal and social relations are not threatened by affirmative action may be quite supportive of such policies as a way of creating healthy environments for various kinds of economic activities. The greatest resistance to affirmative action seems to come from those sectors whose jobs and personal and social relations with blacks and other people of color may be threatened. Leaders of the metropolitan establishment do not really care if city workers, fire and police officials, blue collar workers and secretaries are black, or if lower level white workers are forced to accept blacks as co-workers, as long as a healthy economic environment is not at risk. These same leaders may be concerned about affirmative action among white collar workers, insofar as their own personal and social relations with blacks may change. But, as long as the foundations built in the last three or four decades are not threatened, leaders of the metropolitan establishment could very easily support institutional access for blacks.

It seems that, in some American cities, demographic and political developments have forced the owners and managers of the powerful corporations to support greater access for blacks in the primary labor market. In places like Atlanta and Detroit, for example, some black leadership and some of the corporate sector have developed an alliance of sorts. In Atlanta, the black community may have exchanged its "structural" threat to the business community for access to labor market opportunities in the private and public sectors. In this particular city, the black community's potential threat to economic stability is based on their numbers and proportion of the total city's population, and the kind of political questions its leadership could possibly raise around social and economic concerns. As the black population increases in American cities, and black leaders explore various kinds of political strategies for the benefit of their constituencies, the owners and managers of wealth and their governmental colleagues (e.g., popularly elected mayors and legislators) will concede the importance of access for people of color; it is in their political and economic interests to do so. But affirmative action will still be resisted by poor and working class whites, who perceive access threatening, not only to their economic well-being, but also to their social and personal relations.

The way mayoral candidate Mel King introduced affirmative action and other related issues of access introduces a new development in the urban polity's contests for power. "Access," in Mel King's mayoral platform, reflected a package of public policy goals. One of these related goals was access to jobs in Boston's private and public sectors. Another was physical access. Mel King was the only candidate who aggressively called for the right of blacks to walk and live in any neighborhood in Boston. None of the other major candidates offered to make this a major issue. But Mel King did not blame physical and economic inaccessibility for blacks on working-class or middle-class whites. He continually called upon leaders in power to accept their public and moral responsibility to make Boston liveable for everyone. Mel King argued during both mayoral campaigns that leaders in the private sector, or in religion, had as much responsibility for the quality of life in this city as did public leaders and officials. In the article from *Debate and Understanding*, the authors stated that the politics Mel King represented were in fact an extension of the late Dr. King's philosophy.[14] Mel King argued that access would not be effective if the relationship between the powerful and wealthy and the powerless in Boston were to remain the same. Thus, access alone, and related issues like affirmative action, are not enough to nurture a healthy social and economic environment for everyone. It is no longer enough for the business, religious and educational leadership to support affirmative action as mere reform to assist businesses in the pursuit of profits. Healthy social and economic conditions conducive for the survival of cities can no longer be achieved with public policy pursued within a moral vacuum or in ways which do not redistribute power. The only way interests with power and wealth can develop socially viable relations with blacks and the poor is by seeking policies directly aimed at the elimination of racism and poverty—this will require a redistribution of power.

The kind of access issues which the metropolitan establishment must pursue, in the interests of profits and social health, must include the objective interests of poor and working class whites. Corporate America could generate a social atmosphere of racial and ethnic cooperation by pursuing policies which seek to share society's resources in more equitable ways. But this will not occur, unless blacks representing their communities can obtain enough power and influence to participate fully in public and private decision-making procedures which determine how people live and behave toward each other.

The Mel King for Mayor campaigns also brought into Boston's electoral arena not only actors who were attracted to the issues which King raised, but also those disaffected from traditional electoral processes. New electoral actors supported the kind of activism which was based in large part upon earlier political, educational and community struggles for justice and equality in Boston. As black politics in Boston evolved from what Mel King described as the "Service Stage" to the "Institutional Stage," the kinds of electoral strategies and political approaches utilized by blacks also began to change in this city. As Mel King writes:

> The efforts to get jobs, decent education and other basic American opportunities were all focused on the services offered by churches, social service agencies, settlement houses, charity groups and "concerned" business and commercial groups. We did not see clearly the dependence and debilitation which a service relationship creates. We did not understand that as long as we waited for others to help us, we would never be able to take charge of our own lives. We always assumed that our inability to get access was due to our own inadequacies; our schools weren't good, so our skills were not up to standards, so our family life was inadequate. We did not understand, for instance, that in many cases it was not our children who were inadequate, but the deliberate segregative and discriminatory policies of the Boston School Committee which kept black youngsters from achieving excellence."[15]

Blacks in Boston do understand this now; there are continual organizational experiments with structures and organizations pursuing political power for the new participants.

This kind of political realization led to the birth of activist organizations like the Black Political Task Force, the Black United Front, Blacks for Empowerment and the Rainbow Coalition in Boston. In this city, black activists are utilizing the electoral arena to pursue three important political objectives;

1. provide forums by which to exchange information about political issues; this is especially important considering the lack of black ownership or control in media institutions;
2. develop political sophistication and skills necessary to confront those with power, information and organization; and
3. crystalize the political and social issues which are most pressing and help develop a better understanding of relevant and effective strategies to achieve healthy urban life conditions for all people.

The struggle for control of the mayorship in 1979 and in 1983 has culminated in a city which has been put on notice, politically. It is still difficult for blacks or for people of color to walk safely in most of Boston's neighborhoods. Except for a few secretaries, blacks are seldom seen or heard in the corridors of power in Boston. Large institutions in the fields of health, education and media have yet to open doors to the black community. Despite a few more attempts today, the corporate sector still pursues business in ways which seek to keep blacks in their economic and social "places."

From an optimistic perspective, this matters not, because there is a new mood in Boston; there is a new political mood in large cities across America with sizeable black populations. There is a new sense of pride in black America. And there is a *new* sense of political urgency as well. This is why, despite Ronald Reagan's victory on November 6, 1984, blacks still felt they had won something. Blacks (and most Americans) knew Reagan would probably win the election. But the black electorate still turned out in large numbers against the president, his policies, and his mentality. Blacks have put America on notice. The black community is ready to seek change for the benefit of all Americans again. Blacks and their allies in Latino and white communities of Boston won the "real" election in 1983. Perhaps the most powerful and prescient moment of the mayoral campaign was the night of the election, when thousands of people, young, old, black, white and yellow, marched together on City Hall, chanting: "The people united, shall not be defeated." As black political power grows in Boston, and as citizen support for a progressive public policy agenda grows, racism, poverty and sexism will be weakened. And the people, institutions and values which support the suppression of the human spirit will also be weakened.

Notes

1. The term "urban executive coalition" is borrowed from Robert H. Salisbury, "The New Convergence of Power in Urban Politics", *Journal of Politics*, November, 1964.
2. Michael Harrington, *The Twilight of Capitalism*, Simon and Schuster, New York, p. 223.
3. *Ibid.*, p. 327.
4. On this idea, see Francis F. Piven and Richard Cloward, "What Chance for Black Power?", *Politics of Turmoil*, Vintage Books, New York, 1969, p. 261.
5. Martin Luther King, Jr. *Where Do We Go From Here: Chaos or Community?*, Beacon Press, Boston, MA 1967, p. 186.
6. *Focus*, September, 1984.
7. *Race, Reform and Rebellion: The Second Reconstruction in Black America, 1945-1982*, University Press of Mississippi, Jackson, MS, 1984, p. 194.

8. *The New York Times*, "A Party of Access?", November 25, 1984, p. E 17.
9. James Boggs, *Racism and the Class Struggle*, Monthly Review Press, New York, 1970, p. 12.
10. *Who Governs*, Yale University Press, New Haven, CT, 1961.
11. Norman I. Farnstein and Susan S. Farnstein, *Urban Political Movements: The Search for Power by Minority Groups in American Cities*, Prentice-Hall, Inc., NJ, 1973, p. xiii.
12. *The New York Times*, October 29, November 1, 4, 5 and 21, 1983.
13. See Peter Bachrach and Merton S. Baratz *Power and Poverty: Theory and Practice*, Oxford University Press, New York, 1970, p. 47-48.
14. James Jennings and Melvin I. King, "Boston: Chaos or Community?", *Debate and Understanding*, Summer, 1983.
15. *Chain of Change*, South End Press, Boston, MA, 1980, p. xxvi.

Index

Ackerman, Barbara, 50
Alberts, Rev. William, 64
Alioto, Mayor Joseph, 80
Ansara, Michael, 122–123
Arlook, Ira, 122
Asians, right to political representation, 8, precincts in 1983 mayoral election, 103–105, ties with Mel King, 129–131
Atkins, Thomas, 66, mayoral candidate, 70, elected to city council seat, 110, challenges Mayor White, 112–113

Banks, Lawrence, 16–18
Barnicle, Mike, 142
Bartley, David, 27
Batson, Ruth, 28
Beame, Abraham, 59
Black Political Task Force, 5–6, as community organization, 32–33, 117, objects to district boundaries, 67
Bolling, Royal, Jr., 27–29
Bolling, Royal, Sr., 27–29, 114
Bonner-Lyons, Patricia, 113
Boston Globe, The, criticizes White administration, 62, supports Ray Flynn, 104, 137–172
Boston Herald, The, 62, 156
Bradley, Tom, 53
Bunte, Doris, elected to Mass. House of Reps., 27, confronts Mayor White, 36, board member to Boston Housing Authority, 63, aligns with RAP, 81
Burnham, Margaret, 31

Carey, Gov. Hugh, 60
Carthan, Mayor Eddie James, 175, 184
Catlin, Ephron, 107
Clarke, Hubert, 15
Clark, Kenneth, 91
Collins, John, 108
Curley, Mayor James Michael, 13–15, loses to Hynes, 107–109, administration of, 128–129

Daniels, John, 12, 74
DiGrazia, Robert, 28
Dooley, Ray, 126
Dorchester Community News, 123–124
Doyle, John, 149
Douglass, Frederick, 39
DuBois, W.E.B., 39
Dukakis, Michael, 40–50

Evers, Medgar, 109
Etzioni, Amitai, 91

Fantini, Mario, 145
Farrakhan, Louis, 185

Finfer, Lew, 104
Finnegan, David, 35, as mayoral candidate, 100–103, criticizes Flynn campaign strategy, 142–143
Fitzgerald, Mayor John H., 12
Flaherty, Rep. Michael, 148
Flynn, Mayor Ray, white liberal support of, 6, background, 99–100, support of ROAR, 114, and hiring quotas, 120, mayoral campaign, 122–131, 137–172
Frost, Robert, 63

Garcia, Frieda, 71
Garrity, Judge Arthur W., and court-ordered busing, 113, 147–148
Garvey, Marcus, 39
Gibbs, Kay, 28
Germond, Jack, 138, 153
Glazer, Nathan, 40
Glynn, Dennis, 16–17
Gray, Irving, 16
Green, Roger, 175

Harrison, William E., 17
Hatch, Edward, 48, 51
Healy, Robert, 138, 142–143
Hicks, Louise Day, 27, 65, mayoral campaign, 70–71, 77, 101, school committee chairman, 109, loses mayoral race, 110–116, against busing, 124, 143
Hill, Adelaide, 19
Hill, Arthur D., 12
Hiller, Andy, 163–164

Houghton, Alfred, 15
Hynes, John, 107

Jackson, Rev. Jesse, criticizes media, 154–155, effects of presidential campaign, 175, campaign for president, 1, 137, 179–185, supports Mel King, 104
Johnson, Ralph "Fats", 16
Jones, Hubert, 1, 27
Jordan, David, 13, 20
Jordan, Robert A., 70, 157, 160

Kelley, Rev. R.D., 139
Kelly, James M., 102, 146, 157–159
Kennedy, Charles, 139
Kenney, David A., 15–17
Kent, Sandy, 164
Kerrigan, John, 113, 143
Kierstead, Robert, 162
Kiley, Robert, 140–142
King, Edward J., 50–51
King, Rev. Martin Luther, Jr., 37, 168, 185, assassination aftermath, 111, Boston appearance, 109, *Where Do We Go From Here?*, 90–98, 177–178
King, Melvin, *Chain of Change*, 116, 131, Mayoral Campaign, 1–2, 5–6, 11, 33–37, 41, 45, 48, 63, 69, 75–76, 80–82, 89–98, 113, Rainbow Coalition, 99–132, School Committee, 109, State Representative, 32, 45, 52, 60, 113
Kozol, Jonathan, *Death at an Early Age*, 109

Landsmark, Theodore, 146–147, 159
Latinos, 97, and housing issue, 122–124, political participation in, 8, 60, 66–71, 78–79, 111–112, 171, 184, supports Mel King, 103–105, 129–130, 140
Loftin, Harry, 15
Logue, Ed, 108
Loring, John, 29

McGuire, Jean, 118
McIlviane, John, 17
Mahoney, Jim, 164
Malcolm X, 39, 185
Marable, Manning, 40, 179
May, Owen, 164
Medeiros, Cardinal Humberto, 150, 164
Menzies, Ian, 137–138, 170
Merritt, Robert, 18–19
Miller, Mel, 27
Moakley, John, 27
Mondale, Walter, 178–181
Mouton, Mayor Barbara, 175
Moynihan, Pat, 40
Murphy, William, 175

NAACP, 18, 111, 146, and busing crisis, 113, community involvment, 20, sues BHA, 108
Nelson, Joseph, 14–15
Newport, Mayor Gus, 175
Nussbaum, Karen, 123
Nyhan, David, 137–138, 154, 169, 171–172

O'Bryant, John, 32, seat on Boston School Committee, 66, 117–118
O'Neil, Albert, 157
Otwell, Ralph, 11
Owens, Bill, 27–29, 62, 77, 114–116

Palladino, Elvira Pixie, 157
Parks, Paul, 81
Poleet, Richard, 147, 159
Powers, John, 108

Reagan, Pres. Ronald, 179–181, 190
Renfro, Diane, 28
Richardson, Martin P., 15
Riley, Rev. S.M., Jr., 14
Roberts, Simeon, 16
Robinson, Rev. John, 163
Robinson, Walter V., 159–160
Rushing, Byron, 19, 41
Ryan, Charlotte, 124

Saltonstall, Leverett, 4, 15–16
Scharfenberg, Kirk, 141–142
Schrag, Peter, 109
Scondras, David, 118
Smith, Maurice, 16–16
South Boston Tribune, 145–148, 156
Sparrow, William S., 16
Spence, Harry, 121
Spring, Micho, 64
Storin, Matthew V., 162
Studley, Edward, 157–159
Sullivan, Daniel, 15–17
Szep, Paul, 154

Taylor, Shag, 14–19
Taylor, William O., 162–164
Teixeira, Ray, 16
Timility, Joseph, 35, 52, 65, 115
Trotter, William Monroe, 12
Turner, Robert L., 137–140, 143, 161

Vann, Al, 175
Vennochi, Joan, 154, 160–163

Washington, Booker T., 39
Washington, Edith, 18
Wasington, Mayor Harold, 1, 104–105, 139–140, 171, 175, 184
Watson, Tom, 127
Weinstock, Ed, 164

White, Mayor Kevin H., 4, 30, 137, 145, 168, mayoral campaign, 35–36, 52; relations with black community, 110–121, 128, 151–158, term as mayor, 57–81, 100–106
Williams, Darryl, 139, 150
Williams, Lillian, 18
Wilson, William, 39–40, 73
Winegar, Jerome, 143–151, 157
Winship, Thomas, 162
Witcover, Jules, 138, 153
Wolff, James G., 12
Woodlief, Wayne, 156–159
Worthy, Mabel, 18

Yancey, Charles, 118
Young, Mayor Andrew, 104–105